✔ KU-786-894

Margaret Hennig and Anne Jardim

The Managerial Woman

POCKET BOOKS

New York   London   Toronto   Sydney   Tokyo   Singapore

Excerpts from *The Adolescent Experience* by Elizabeth Douvan and Joseph
Adelson. Copyright © 1966 by John Wiley & Sons, Inc. Reprinted by permis
sion of John Wiley & Sons, Inc.

POCKET BOOKS, a division of Simon & Schuster Inc.
1230 Avenue of the Americas, New York, NY 10020

ISBN: 0-671-67431-5

First Pocket Books printing July 1978

20 19 18 17 16 15 14 13

POCKET and colophon are registered trademarks of
Simon & Schuster Inc.

Printed in the U.S.A.

A LANDMARK BOOK—THE ESSENTIAL SURVIVAL MANUAL

Drs. Margaret Hennig and Anne Jardim received their doctoral degrees from Harvard Business School. They are consultants to a number of major corporations and are joint directors of the Graduate Program in Management for women which they founded at Simmons College in 1973. They lecture throughout the country, and have been the focus of major reportage in *Time, Business Week, The New York Times, New York, The Chicago Tribune,* and many other publications.

"May become **the definitive book** for female 'managers' on many levels." —*Glamour*

"**A must** for women who are managers or who want to be, and for the men who supervise or work with talented women."
—John D. Moorhead,
Christian Science Monitor

"Provides **a plan of action** for women who aspire to business advancement."
—*King Features Syndicate*

FOR EVERY WOMAN INTERESTED IN GETTING INTO —AND SURVIVING—THE LAND OF THE BOSSES

Contents

Dr. Margaret Hennig and Dr. Anne Jardim received their doctorates from the Harvard Business School. They currently serve as consultants to a number of business and women's professional organizations and are the joint founders and directors of the Simmons College Graduate Program in Management, a master's program designed for women.

Preface

This book is the outcome of research jointly begun by its authors in 1973. Moving from Margaret Hennig's findings on women executives in her 1970 doctoral thesis, the research encompasses a wider spectrum of women in management—their assumptions, perceptions and behavior; men in management and the organizational environment; and real and potential outcomes for both men and women in terms of career achievement.

Of the book's three parts, Anne Jardim is responsible for writing Part I and Margaret Hennig for writing Part III. Part II is drawn from Margaret Hennig's doctoral thesis which has been adapted for publication by the authors. The theoretical issues raised and the reformulations presented in Chapters 4 and 11 represent a continuation of Anne Jardim's earlier work on psychoanalytic approaches to managerial behavior.

The authors are more than usually indebted to others in making this book a reality, in particular to Patricia Kosinar and Catherine Campbell Bradley, with whom they have worked from the beginning. To Bonnie Marett and Jeanne Deschamps Stanton. To Mary Ann Chase-Borden, Gretchen Gerzina, Jenny Hedlund and Jennie King. And to men and women in management in companies across the country whose experience permitted the insights and helped form the conclusions reflected in the text.

What this book is about

Many readers will begin this book saying, "Yes, yes, very interesting subject, but things have changed. Women are equal now and why belabor the point in a book? After all, we are almost a decade into the women's movement. The civil rights act is more than ten years old, and the resulting executive orders deal directly with, and enforce, equal employment opportunity for women. And surely today's generation of women is far more capable of dealing with the problems that confronted women in the past. And certainly the law has given them the widest possible opportunity to do what they really want."

If we accept this simple summary of the present we will not see what this book is really about, for the problems are not so simple, nor at a deeper level have things changed all that much.

There is little doubt that the legal drive to enforce equal opportunity has succeeded in making American organizations more aware of women both in blue-collar and managerial jobs. Simultaneously, the women's movement has heightened women's awareness of themselves, their rights and their work situations. There is even some evidence that more women now hold management positions than they did ten years ago, yet the most recent statistics show that while women make up 39 per cent of the labor force, less than 5 per cent of those earning more than $10,000 a year in the census category of Officials, Managers and Proprietors are women. Stated another way, men make up 61 per cent of the labor force, yet 95 per cent of the jobs in this census category paying more than $10,000 are held by men. At higher salary levels —$25,000 and above—the representation of women falls even lower—to 2.3 per cent versus 97.7 per cent for men. In absolute numbers only 11,000 women managers in the United States earn more than $25,-000—in comparison with 449,000 men.[1] If these numbers represent all that equal employment opportunity can provide they are disappointing to say the least. Why are they so small? The explanation lies at least in part in the concepts on which the equal opportunity laws are based. These laws legislate for equal opportunity. They do not and cannot legislate truly equal access to that opportunity, and most important, they cannot ensure that people who have traditionally been discriminated against will immediately and automatically demonstrate the ability to take advantage of whatever access to opportunity may exist.

At the same time there is a real and growing reaction to the enforcement of equal opportunity. It comes from those whose opportunities have been cut back in order to provide room for the inclusion of the newly legitimized outsiders. These people who must make room for the newcomers are becoming hurt, angry, resentful. While law controls formal structure, the implementation of its well-intended thrust must take place through the mechanisms of the informal structure. And in industry that informal structure is populated almost entirely by men, the same men whose opportunities have now been curtailed.

In most organizations the informal system of relationships finds both its origins and present function in the male culture and in the male experience. Its forms, its rules of behavior, its style of communication and its mode of relationships grow directly out of the male developmental experience. This cannot be viewed as either good or bad. It is real. Men founded and developed the vast majority of the organizations we know. Men made them places where they could work and live and their settings were intended to be both comfortable and familiar. And if organizations in general are dominated by a male culture, then we need to note that at the management level, and particularly in its higher ranks, the informal system is truly a bastion of the male life-style.

If we think of the men who belong to these informal systems as the insiders: people who understand and support each other, the structure, and the rules; people who share common aspirations and dreams; people who grew up with similar backgrounds; who played together, learned together, competed together; and concurrently we think of how differently women grow up: their different orientations, expectations, aspirations and experiences—then we can begin to understand why in spite of the law, very little may really have changed for women.

In fact, we can begin to understand why, if threatened by law that either they welcome the outsiders into their midst or be punished for failure to do so, the insiders can make their system work so as to avoid either outcome entirely.

What makes this particularly threatening to the future of women in management is that the informal system is at the heart of the middle management function and grows still more critical with every step upward. Few women are a part of this system and most women don't even recognize it exists. Thus a picture emerges in which those people whom we have called the insiders operate knowledgeably and carefully within a system whose membership typically excludes women; a system about which few women know anything very useful; and because it is a system, which reacts to threats to its members by functioning in such a way as to make it even more difficult for women to become a part of it.

Another way of grasping this complex issue is to consider the often quoted statement about the Black movement: "You can legislate against segregation but you cannot legislate integration." In other words, saying a person cannot be kept out doesn't ensure that that person can get in, and more important, stay in. Beliefs, attitudes and assumptions which people have about themselves and each other and their resulting willingness or unwillingness to accept each other are untouched by law. At another level, there is the critical issue of competence. Unless people not only are, but *believe* that they are, equally able or competent to compete, they will not willingly or successfully integrate themselves with more powerful individuals and groups.

In order to take advantage of equal opportunity women must believe they are, and in fact must be, as competent as their male counterparts. In-depth competence in their chosen field has traditionally been one of women's outstanding strengths, almost an employment characteristic, but competence as a manager requires understanding and skill at working in and with the informal system of relationships in which management jobs are embedded. Such competence represents a stage which most women in organizations have not yet reached, and the guarantee of equal opportunity is empty unless opportunities are created for women to acquire the knowledge and skill which will make it possible for them to understand, to enter and to compete within the informal systems of middle management. Real integration will take place when the outsider group feels strong enough and competent enough to choose to integrate—and when the system which receives them is as aware of this as they.

The laws mandating equal opportunity were desperately needed. They provided the impetus for change. What we now face is a second phase in which consolidation and disintegration of what has so far been achieved are both potential outcomes—and disintegration carries by far the higher costs. If we recognize that laws alone will not ensure that women who aspire to careers in management—and who have the potential to be effective managers—will necessarily succeed, then clearly much more has to be done. The ability to take advantage of equal opportunity is the critical starting point and it has less to do with technical knowledge and much more to do with fundamental differences in perception which stand in the way of acquiring new and necessarily very different skills—differences which have left women trapped in supervisory positions and too often branded as lacking in management potential.

The primary aim of this book is to help men and women understand the critically different beliefs and assumptions which they hold about themselves and each other, about organizations and a management career. These differences result in different styles, different emphases and very different ways of responding to typical management situations on a day-to-day basis. Men understand their own mind-sets but not those of women. The reverse is equally real and the outcome only too often is confusion, misunderstanding and misinterpretation.

As a counterpoint, this book looks at the life and career histories of twenty-five women who by 1970 had reached top management positions in business and industry. At first glance, their stories demonstrate that even without legal pressures to aid them women can build extremely successful management careers. More thoughtful analysis reveals the price they paid —until their mid-thirties their personal lives were mortgaged to pay for their careers.

These women all came from unusual family backgrounds and they first went to work in an unusual decade, the thirties. They moved into middle management amid the unusual strains of World War II. They were able to understand and work effectively in a man's world, and they were ultimately able to do so with a sense of self-worth and personal success. We can learn a great deal from them, not least that the price they paid may be too high for both women *and* men.

How to learn from them, how to change? How to seek change in men's assumptions and attitudes, and in the structure of organizational life itself for those things about women that cannot be changed? These are the questions. The number of women at work is rising annually. The number of women who are heads of households is also rising. The number of women who want more out of work than a survival-level job is increasing significantly. Yet changing deep-rooted and no longer questioned assumptions, present perceptions and behavior is in itself no easy task. How do you even begin?

In the final section of this book we have tried to be

as specific as we can. There is a cluster of issues which women in management jobs do not recognize, interpret and act on in the same way as men. They are all career-related issues, emerging out of organizations built and traditionally managed by men. They are part of the culture, part of the system of relationships, part of the language. And if we have our priorities straight, it would seem that women first and foremost need to learn them. Having learned them, whether they want to act on them is a question of individual choice.

In the past three years we have traveled more than a hundred thousand miles around the United States. In that time we have taught undergraduate women and women at the graduate level, and we have conducted in-depth interviews with more than one hundred women managers in the utilities, banking and communications industries. We have led or been involved in leading more than one hundred one-and-a-half-day career planning seminars with groups of up to thirty women managers at a time. This experience has given us an extensive data base on these three thousand women. We have led seminars for more than one thousand male managers who are responsible for the identification and promotion of women in their companies. In our role as corporate consultants we have worked with top managers to establish policy and develop strategies for the implementation of equal employment opportunity and we have designed total corporate programs to achieve upward mobility for women taking into precise account the critical need to incorporate men in middle management into the overall corporate effort.

The insights we have often painfully won are presented in this book.

PART I

1

The Way It Is: Men and Women in Management Jobs

In the spring of 1973, the authors of this book began a series of in-depth interviews with women who held management positions in a large northeastern public utility. We interviewed forty-five of the company's most senior women managers and by the fall of that year we had extended the project to include sixty-three women who held management positions in the banking industry. Their positions ranged from acting president of a medium-sized bank in the West to the co-founder and joint owner of a bank of her own in the Midwest, to vice-presidents, assistant vice-presidents and cashiers of large urban and small rural banks in the West, Midwest and East. The ages of the women interviewed ranged from twenty-seven to fifty-eight, and with one exception they had worked almost continuously since leaving school or college. The exception was a woman with a family to support who at the age of fifty was accepted into the management training program of a large Midwestern bank, completed the eighteen-month program in eight months and was, when we interviewed her, a vice-president responsible for public relations.

When we began the interviews we were both on the faculty of Harvard Business School, Margaret Hennig as a Visiting Associate Professor on sabbatical leave from Simmons College to teach a course of her own design on women in industry, and Anne Jardim as a member of the faculty in Business Policy.

At the very beginning of that year we had both become advisers to the Business School's Women Students' Association. As we worked with these women we grew more and more concerned at the situation in which many of them found themselves, and we became equally concerned at the lack of response from the school's administration. For example, of the many hundred case studies which a student must analyze and solve in the course of the Harvard M.B.A. program's two years, the merest handful included women. When women *were* included they were often depicted as "problems" with which the hard-pressed male executive unfortunately had to deal. To counter this not so subtle put-down, the women students suggested that the names in existing case studies be changed so that both men and women might see, and have to work with, women acting with authority and responsibility in business situations which demanded intelligence, competence and a decision-making capacity. This suggestion was dismissed as impractical.

The difficulties which the women encountered in the classroom were left to them to solve as best they could. Many women found it hard to participate in class as fully as the case method of teaching required. This was as much because of their own doubts as to whether they could or even wanted to compete with the men in the class, as it was due to the response they received when they did participate. One women told us that she had survived with her male peers by deciding that if she said something intelligent in one class she would balance it by saying nothing in the next, then asking questions and appearing very tentative in the third and then finally risking another intelligent statement in the fourth. Other women found it difficult to deal with the way in which men in their classes acknowledged and built on each other's statements and ignored the women's: a woman student who made a number of critical points in her class analysis only too often found that the man who followed her picked up the discussion where the last man left off and what she had worked painfully hard to achieve was made to seem irrelevant and worthless.

By the spring of that year when we began our series of interviews with women who were already in management jobs, it was clear to us that something needed to be done both for and with women, who as a fractional minority in the male establishment which Harvard Business School epitomized, found themselves confronted by difficulties a good way beyond the ordinary day-to-day problems with which their male counterparts had to deal. The women students at Harvard Business School had to face the same academic problems as their male peers—and then more.

But while we could see that something needed to be done we were not at all sure what it was. What were the deeper issues involved? We got nowhere with blanket explanations such as "a lack of self-confidence" or "achievement versus femininity," or "women fear success." To be at all useful the issues had to be defined a great deal more carefully. What did being a woman in such an environment mean? Could it be that the premises on which the learning process was assumed to be based were so closely tied to the male experience that a woman lacking that experience was at a critical disadvantage? What *did* a woman bring with her and how consequently would she act?

It was against this background in the spring of 1973 that our series of in-depth interviews with women managers began. We hoped at the start that these older and far more experienced women, many of whom were successful in men's terms, would give us a clear understanding of what the underlying problems were, what could be done—because they had done it—to overcome the difficulties we had seen in the Business School's women students.

We built the interviews around each woman's career —when and why she had joined the organization; what she had had to learn and how she had done it; what the blocks were, what the facilitators were; who had helped, who had hindered and why; and what the critical decisions were in both personal and career terms that each had had to make along the way.

By our twentieth interview clear patterns had emerged and they were sustained with varying degrees of emphasis by nearly all of the women. The patterns had little to do with our questions. They had everything to do with what as women they had brought with them to their jobs.

Typically the career decision had been made late, at the age of thirty to thirty-three, "when suddenly I realized I was probably going to have to work for the rest of my life."

In some cases it was a sudden realization that one liked one's work and that it had a much more permanent meaning than something done to pass the time while waiting for something better. In these cases an unexpected acknowledgment by a superior of the quality of her work tended to be the career catalyst for the individual woman. Suddenly she realized that she worked certainly because she needed to, but more than that, she liked what she was doing. She wanted to think of it as an essential part of her future.

The problem was that the great majority had worked continuously since leaving school or college, and in our minds there was a persistent question: What had they failed to see, think about and act on in the preceding ten years? During those critical years in the twenties men are typically attempting to build the foundations of their careers. But if these women were not thinking of the long-term at all, what had they missed? How in spite of it had they got where they were? When we asked this question the answers varied from "I was good at my work and it just happened," to "I was just lucky—someone left at a critical point and they asked me to act," to "I had a boss who believed I could do it," to variations on "I was dragged kicking and screaming up the ladder."

Somehow it had happened. Even thinking back as we asked them to, there was little they could remember that varied the essentially passive theme. They had worked hard and they had had the luck to be chosen.

Yet almost all of these women had some idea of where they wanted to be in five years' time. Some could discuss it in terms of a specific job, others in terms of levels of responsibility and salary. When we asked them what they thought would be critical in achieving what they wanted, however, another pattern emerged. The critical factors they identified were all closely related to their own individual capacities and they were all factors which the women themselves could control or attempt to control. They cited, for example, consistently hard work, outstanding performance, the achievement of higher levels of job competence and further training, either in-house or through college programs and courses. Then there were behavioral factors which they talked about in the following terms—developing greater self-confidence, becoming more aggressive, more effectively delegating work presently done by themselves. Some went further and identified the need for a back-up person whom they could train to take over their current jobs as they themselves moved up.

None of them talked about the organizational environment, an area in which the ability to control outcomes in far less certain. None of them talked of the need to make what they wanted known to people who mattered, of the need to win the support of bosses, peers *and* subordinates, of the need to know as much as one could of the political system, of the need for visibility and its risks. None seemed to recognize that if one is not "seen" by others as the kind of person who should have a particular job all the competence in the world would not get it for them. Again we asked ourselves—if these issues were not even raised, was it likely that on the job, day to day, they would even be acted on? If they *were* acted on, would action be set in the long-term context of "I need this because it could affect my career in this organization three years (or two, or four) from now?" Or would acting on any of these issues be tied to a here and now, get-this-particular-job-done frame of reference? Again, what would they miss if they acted only in terms of the here and now, what would they fail to see and what would be the career cost of not seeing?

Later, we were to see example after example of the costs involved in non-recognition of the environment and the consequent failure to build it into career aspirations over the long-term. These women gave us a first understanding of this pattern. Acted out by a woman executive in her early thirties in a large New York company it looked like this: This woman earned $28,000 a year. She was bright, competent and aggressive. She gave every indication of knowing where she wanted to go. She moved from a position as manager in computer systems at the request of the company's executive vice-president into an eighteen-month assignment to take over development of action programs for women: career counseling, career planning, management training, internships and attachment programs. As a means of achieving visibility quickly and of becoming known to the most senior levels of management as a person of clear intelligence who could be of genuine help to them, the position and how she filled it could tangibly affect her future career.

She had been on the job for six months, and in a difficult and often ambiguous situation (her reporting relationships were not as clear as they might have been and her liaison with men in management on the issues she was responsible for was not easy), she had nonetheless achieved a measurable level of success. At this point we met with her and with the executive vice-president, an informal and exceptionally perceptive man, to discuss progress to date. It was late on a Monday afternoon. The executive vice-president followed the discussion closely, raised a number of important questions and was clearly committed to making the programs succeed. Finally he said to her, "I think we now have enough behind us to justify a presidential policy statement to the organization. We can identify what has worked, explain why and how it has worked and show what we still need to do. If you give me a draft by Friday I can discuss it with the president when I see him over the weekend." For a moment she looked staggered and then she said, "I can't. I'm going to an out-of-state conference on Friday." He looked at her and then said very carefully, "Well, I wouldn't object to having it on Thursday." She said, "But the problem is, I'm making a presentation at the conference and there are a lot of visuals involved. I'm going down on Thursday to rehearse the whole thing." He said, "Then make it Wednesday." She said, "But tomorrow is Tuesday and I've got everything on my desk to clear up before I go." He said, "Look, it doesn't really matter *how* you arrange this, I *want* that draft by Friday."

The meeting ended and we left the room with her. She was upset by what had happened. "Can you believe," she said to us, "that this company is taking the women's issue seriously? Did you hear him? Drop everything. Forget about priorities. Do what I say! And it's a draft, for God's sake!"

We asked her if she had any idea of what she had been offered—and hadn't heard. She had in effect been told that her work so far had been of a high enough standard to merit a presidential stamp of approval. Translated into official company policy, what she had set out to achieve would now become a stated objective for every company manager. Over the next year this meant that her position would be solidified in the eyes of the management men with whom she had to deal and her job made that much simpler. The possibility existed that she might have to meet with the president to discuss the draft and so become a face with a name and a clear competence. Was that worth anything in the long-run? She looked stunned. She said, "My God, I never saw it."

It is in interactions such as this, where perception must be translated into behavior and response, that the difficulty lies. She "never saw it." *It* relates to a career concept which has to do with advancement, with growth in status and influence as well as in skill and expertise. Much more a man's career concept than a woman's, its implications for day-to-day perception, behavior and misunderstanding are immense.

2

Patterns of Difference and Their Implications

If we start running our series of findings together, all of them linked to difference in the concept of a career, a distinct picture emerges. First there is the late career decision, with career decision defined as a conscious commitment to advancement over the long term. It is a decision a woman typically makes some ten years into her "career" and to that point, equally typically, there is a manifest concentration on the day-to-day aspects of the job with no viable concept of time in relation to oneself to back it up, to measure progress, or to allow one to adapt or change direction, which a job seen as the beginning of a career over time would provide: "After all, I may not even be working when I'm thirty."

Second, there is the sense of passivity, "It just happened—somebody did it for me," which effectively blocks the ability to move freely between successful past experience—what the individual has learned about her own strengths—and the demands of a new situation. Past experience if recalled passively discounts strengths and obscures initiatives which then have to be rediscovered over and over again as situations arise. This makes it difficult to predict mastery in the future of what one may well have been able to master in the past, and that difficulty fosters doubts and anxieties which then appear to be the central issue to be coped with: "How do I become more self-confident, more aggressive?"

Third, there is the emphasis on individual self-improvement as the critical factor determining career advancement. This in itself is related to the sense of passivity, to the overwhelming sense of "waiting to be chosen." It depends for its rationale upon a belief in the effectiveness of the formal structure, formal definitions, roles, policies, the way things should be, and what it critically omits is a sense of the organizational environment—the informal system of relationships and information sharing, ties of loyalty and of dependence, of favors granted and owed, of mutual benefit, of protection—which men unfailingly and invariably take into account to however greater or lesser a degree. When the formal structure fails to respond as it should, the individual who has relied on it is often left hopelessly disappointed and immobilizingly unable to accept that the influence of the informal system is not an exception or an aberration but a continuing element in the organizational process.

These findings emerged from our interviews with just over one hundred women managers, and they provided the basis for a questionnaire which we have since used in two of the seminars we teach, one for management women and the other for management men. With our associates, we have now taught more than three thousand women and more than one thousand men, all of whom have completed the questionnaire and then given us their responses question by question which, put on a blackboard, allow any patterns that emerge to be identified.

Before we even discuss these patterns, however, we want to stress a critical element in how the questionnaire responses are made: they are first off the top of the head responses, first thoughts, first ideas that come to mind. They are habitual responses, reflecting accustomed habits of mind which individuals no longer think twice about, and they help identify only what individual men and women are personally attuned to or not attuned to in the day-to-day course of their jobs. They help identify, *in relation to an individual's concept of his or her career,* what is sensed or not sensed, seen or not seen, heard or not heard, and as a consequence what is acted on or not. The men's patterns of response are strikingly different from the women's. Yet these differences are in no way a measure of intelligence or of actual job competence. Anyone who is determined to interpret the patterns to prove deficiency rather than difference will of course do so, but in doing so will invalidate his or her interpretation by negating the basis on which the responses are made and the relative meaning that attaches to them.

With this as the overriding qualification on how they can validly be used, the differences in response give an extraordinary perspective to the separate worlds of men and women in management.

For example, a question as simple as "What is a job?" With women the pattern of response is that it is what one does day-to-day, nine to five, most often it is routine and tedious, it has to be done, it is a means of survival, of earning a living.

With men the pattern is one of a task to be completed, a set of responsibilities to be met, an assignment or a set of assignments to be fulfilled, a means of support, of earning a living. As a first response the element of compulsion and boredom are notably absent and a job is seen as essentially something to be completed with the underlying meaning that one then goes on to something else. Women's responses lack a sense of temporariness, of the short-term, of movement, of a beginning *and* an end.

The patterns that emerge in definitions of a career are even more striking. Women see a career as personal growth, as self-fulfillment, as satisfaction, as making a contribution to others, as doing what one wants to do. While men indubitably want these things too, when they visualize a career they see it as a series of jobs, a progression of jobs, as a path leading upward with recognition and reward implied. In all of the seminars we have taught we have never once seen a woman refer to recognition or reward as part of her career definition.

It doesn't take very much to start translating these differences in mind-set into the implications they hold for on-the-job behavior. Men expressly relate the jobs they do to their concept of career as advancement, as upward progression. For them a job *is* part of a career. Women separate the two issues completely: a job is in the here and now and a career is an intensely personal goal which the individual alone can judge whether she has achieved. The response of the woman who was unable to have the draft statement ready by Friday becomes explicable: if one's career priorities are set in a context as necessarily vague and difficult of measurement as that of personal growth, for example, one is inevitably thrown back on exceptional performance in the here and now as an overwhelmingly important fact in developing a sense of achievement, and one zeroes in on every detail of the current job. In the process one neither sees nor hears the cues directed at a quite different concept of career, a concept which has to do with how in reality one moves up through a hierarchy of job responsibilities and personal influence. Involved as she was with the job she had, preoccupied with the need to master it, concerned with the here and now rather than with a career "later" defined in terms that men would readily understand, this woman never heard what was really being said to her.

Men to whom we have described this incident find it difficult to believe that anyone would have acted as she did. On one unforgettable occasion we were teaching a seminar for men at the vice-presidential level in the same company. We described the incident changing only the company setting. One man was particularly incredulous. He said that the women he knew in the company would never have acted in this way. He could think of a number of them, but just as an example . . . He named her. During the coffee break he went down to her office, told her what we had said, repeated that he didn't believe it and asked her what she would have done. She told us that she swallowed hard, looked him in the eye and said, "Well, I've seen it happen."

It is as if women see a job in the context of now . . . now . . . now . . . and see a career as some future self-realization far off in the distance. Men, on the other hand, see a job in the context of now and later simultaneously. They see it as part of a career, and as a consequence the cues they see, hear and act on, the relationships they strive to develop and the visibility they seek to achieve have both a present meaning and a future importance.

From a very early age men expect to work to support at least themselves. Only a fractional minority of white women come face to face with this issue as little girls. Instead, for the individual woman the emphasis, expressed or implied, is placed on the need to find someone to support *her*. The difference in mind-set that develops from this crossroads of childhood's expectations and ambitions is enormous. Boys take one road, and most adult men cannot even remember when it was that they first understood that they would have to support themselves and what this meant. The tensions and anxieties that surround the issue are, for boys, directly related to the problems they encounter in the environment: Can they do this, can they master that, are they any good at something else? And always there is the reassurance that men do these things, and have always done them, so at worst if one can't do a particular thing very well there will be something else one *can* do. The road a girl takes conjures up different anxieties, different tensions. Will she find someone to support and look after her? Is she pretty enough, nice enough, clever enough—or too plain or too clever?

From a very early age children fantasize about their futures and the future for a little girl inescapably has a husband in it: at that point her parents are the only model she has. Fathers support wives and children and even where a mother works the father's job is usually seen as the more critical. The little girl looks at the little boys she knows and wonders—would he be a good husband, would he look after her? Would he be nice to her—nicer than her father is to her mother, or as nice? Most important of all, would he choose her? The theme of vicarious independence is very real and the anxieties associated with possible failure have to do with how one looks, with how one seems, with how one appears—*not* with what one can or cannot do.

In the light of this it hardly seems strange that the mind-set of an adult woman, even a woman with a tangible claim to career success, should still bear traces of a different reality—a reality which has far more to do with individual attributes and their effect on others and far less to do with actively engaging the environment. The difficulties which arise for women from the confrontation in a management setting of these two different realities are compounded by an unawareness on the part of both men and women that the differences even exist.

And there are still other patterns. One has to do with the ability to see one's career as an integral part of one's life. Men find it difficult to separate personal goals from career goals. They see one set as dependent on the other and they try to negotiate and to trade off between each set of goals when conflict threatens the balance. Women on the other hand actively strive for separation. They think it through and choose to make the distinction: "My personal life is quite separate from my career and that is how I want it."

While there are real reasons for the drive to maintain this separation, there are painful disadvantages to be coped with as one attempts it. The reasons for separation can range from a need to be a different person at home in order not to threaten a man because one loves or is afraid of him, to a remorseless sense of guilt unless one can simultaneously be a perfect wife, mother or lover. The latter phenomenon hinges on a complicated psychological maneuver which runs something like this: "Given that the role I *should* accept is a woman's role, then I can only justify, rationalize, explain taking on a different role if I'm so good at the woman's role that no one can question it, which then leaves me free to take on the rest."

The net outcome moving from any point on this range of motivation is intentionally the same—one lives two lives. But when one does this how is negotiation possible? How does one trade off between them, how does one balance conflict? If a woman has actively encouraged the individuals who mean a great deal to her to believe that her career life is of little significance to her, *and has consistently acted it out,* how does she get them to believe in, and help her solve, a crisis arising from a serious clash between the two? Typically she can't and in her own eyes she often fails at both. In the meantime in the absence of crisis, her life as a whole is made that much more difficult as she attempts to switch off and on from the person she is in one setting to the person she should be in the other.

Why women tend to make so explicit a separation is a much larger question whose answer lies in the society around us and both men and women explain it in very similar ways: men grow up knowing they will have to work for the rest of their lives, they are expected to, and they prepare for it. They join an organization where career advancement for men is the traditional socially sanctioned norm. However minimally, their ambitions are supported, they are seen as legitimate. A bright young man is a "comer" and even the less bright have to prove by their performance that they do not belong. In effect they have to prove failure. Women on the other hand grow up in a cloud of ambiguity: will they work or won't they? If they do, for how long? Are they expected to or aren't they and for how long? They join an organization where career advancement for women is typically the exception and where, given prior and often articulated assumptions that they don't, they have to prove by their performance that they do belong. In effect they have to prove success, and on a continuous basis. They have to prove, given prior and often articulated assumptions that they will, that their careers will not be dual, discontinuous and consequently marked by a lack of commitment—a burden of proof to which a man is never asked to submit. They tend to feel that their lives *are* dual, that they cannot trade off between the two lives imposed upon them even though the ability to do so might well allow for optimization in both. They begin to feel that survival depends on the separation which both sides of their lives demand.

How many men in management whom you know have family photographs on their desks? How many women in management? Yet for women, as for men, the road to integration runs along small byways like these. Men take them automatically, without even thinking about them, while women consciously assume that they want the opposite. For example, a woman in a direct-mail organization, the only woman in a sales group of twenty-nine men, won her company's 1974 award for highest individual sales. She was thrilled. The 1973 winner, a man she knew quite well, came up to congratulate her. He said that he had had his presentation certificate beautifully framed and he could give her the name of the framer. She said, "Can I come into your office and look at it?" He said, "Well, it isn't there. It's hanging in the family room at home. I'll have to bring it in." She told us the story. He had looked surprised, and she said she remembered thinking, "What's wrong with him, why isn't it in his office? He won it for what he does here. Mine is going to stay here."

We asked her if she could tell us how her husband saw her job, could she describe *his* understanding of what it was she did at work? She found this extremely difficult to do. "Both he and my son know I have a good job. Of course they don't know the details. They know I'm in sales. They know I'm the only woman and the only black in the group." She smiled, "And they know we need the money."

In fact she knew a great deal more about her husband's job than he did of hers. We asked her how she managed if for instance their son were ill. She said that of course she missed work. We were left to wonder whose job in the eyes of both was by far the more important and didn't she continually reinforce this joint perception? We had the feeling that she probably earned as much as her husband did, yet she had a job and he had a career, and both of them saw it that way. We asked her if she could really afford to miss work on a day when she was to meet with a really important client, or attend a really important meeting. That had not happened yet, she said. But if it did? She guessed she could ask her husband to stay. Would he? She'd have to persuade him. What would that involve? She threw up her hands. "I guess I'd have to start right at the beginning and tell him what my job was about, why I had to go and why he had to stay." Would he be more easily persuaded if he were already aware of what her job involved and what it meant to her? She said, very slowly and very thoughtfully, "I think I'll take the award certificate home."

A few months later she wrote us a letter. She had taken her certificate home and had hung it in the family room. She couldn't believe the questions she'd been asked about her job, about the people she worked with, about the company. The questions came from her husband, her son, her friends and her husband's friends.

Still another pattern of difference centers on the concept of personal strategy. Men define this as winning, as achieving a goal or reaching an objective. In discussing this issue they ask a question whose many forms bear the same meaning: What's in it for me? It is a critical question because it allows the future to be brought into consideration. What's in it for me now, attractive as it might be, might well over the long term undermine what I want ultimately to achieve. It is a question that almost inevitably evokes a "Yes, but . . ." answer if one asks it of oneself, and the "but" leads one into the attempt to predict and thus to anticipate future outcomes.

Women's definitions in contrast are definitions of process: planning, finding the best way, the best possible method. The element of time is absent from the examples they give: "In order to get a particular job done I did thus and so." But what about the implications a year from now of doing thus and so? The giver of the example suddenly realizes what she has said. She has described what was for her the best way of resolving a particular problem in the here and now with no consideration given to the way in which that resolution might or might not affect her over time.

Why this happens is again a question that reaches into the past. It focuses on an issue which though fast becoming over-worked is no less valid because of that: sports—the games boys play and men follow. For example:

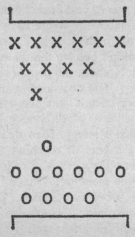

Women's comments attempt to identify what this diagram represents. Is it a game? If so, is it field hockey, football or could it be baseball? How many games need teams of eleven? Are those goal posts?

Men's comments are immediately evaluative: "It's football and it's a lousy play. Change the coach. Switch to another channel."

What lies behind this difference in response begins with small boys learning about teams, about being members of teams, about winning and losing. Their concept of strategy may at first be a very simple one: how you win may mean no more than getting the fat boys on your team so you can trample the skinny boys on the other.

But then it becomes more sophisticated and task specialization sets in. Runners *and* blockers are seen to be needed. The guys with the imagination to plan and anticipate possible outcomes achieve a value of their own. A team makes it possible to become a star and one has to learn how to manage this. A team makes it possible to share a star's luster by active association, and again one can learn how to manage this. A team can even be a place to hide, a place to learn about survival—how to stay on, how to be given another chance; "After all he's too nice a guy to drop!", or "He's not really producing yet but he's learning fast, and he's a real straight player." Over and above this, there is the drive to win and of necessity win as a team, not as a lone individual independent of everyone else.

What do men experience, learn and then internalize as working assumptions from a game like football? And does it matter that the great majority of women share neither their experience nor their assumptions?

Simply as an experience, ask a man you know to

try to think back to the time when he played a team game like football. What was it like? What did he begin to learn? What did he *have* to learn if he wanted to stay on the team?

Varying only as to form, the answers we have been given—time and time again—are:

What was it like? What did you begin to learn?	*What did you have to learn if you wanted to stay on the team?*
It was boys only	Competition, you had to win
Team work	
Hard work	Cooperation to get a job done—you had to work with guys you wouldn't choose as friends outside the team
Preparation and practice, practice, practice	
If you were knocked down you had to get up again	
It gave you a sense of belonging, of being part of something bigger than yourself	If you got swell-headed about how fast you could run then the other guys didn't block for you any more
You learned that a team needs a leader because motivation or lack of it depends on the coach	Losing, what it felt like to lose
	That you win some, you lose some
You learned fast that some people were better than others—but you had to have eleven	How to take criticism—from the coach, your peers, the crowd
	That you didn't get anywhere without planning and you had to have alternative plans
	Once you knew the rules you could bend them—and you could influence the referee

Consider these answers from two points of view: the way they define an environment and the personal skills they identify as needed to survive in it. Do they describe fairly closely a management environment in a corporate setting? Do they reflect skills an effective manager must be able to rely on?

Beyond individual hard work, persistence and the ability to deal with criticism by seeing it as directed much less to the person and much more to task achievement, these answers have to do with goals and objectives; with winning and attempting to deal with loss by distancing it—you win some, you lose some; with group relationships—how to maintain and work with them; and with relationships to authority—whether it be rules or people.

These are personal skills. Boys begin to develop them in an outdoor classroom to which girls traditionally have had no access. After five to fifteen years of practice, men bring these skills with them to management jobs and they are skills critical to job performance once the dividing line between supervision and management is crossed.

Supervision typically involves responsibility for routine, predictable and specific job performance by subordinates in an area of skills with which the supervisor is extremely familiar. He or she usually "grew up" in that skill: learned it when he or she first went to work, performed it well, was promoted to supervise others to do what he or she once did.

Goals and plans to achieve them are usually set for the supervisor to follow. Problems are routine, predictable and can be solved as they arise.

Learning the more technical aspects of the job can be achieved on one's own—seminars, courses, textbooks.

The formal system of relationships required to do

the job is typically vertical—up the line to one's boss, down the line to subordinates.

Crossing the line between supervision and management demands that an individual be prepared for a series of fundamental changes in the skills required to do the job, changes for which no formal training is typically available.

In management jobs, goals and plans to meet them are no longer as clearly set as they were for the supervisor. They are increasingly part of a manager's responsibility. Success at planning demands an awareness of group weakness and strengths and ability to balance the one against the other without destructive conflict. "Some people are better than others but you have to have eleven."

Goal-setting. Planning. But how do you get the plan implemented?

"The team needs a leader because motivation or lack of it depends on the coach." "Knowing the rules and bending them." "Influencing the referee." "Taking criticism from (your own) coach, your peers, the crowd." "Winning *and* losing." "Winning some, losing some."

Another required shift in skills has to do with problem-solving. The supervisor deals with more or less routine day-to-day problems susceptible to more or less tried and true solutions. The manager has to *anticipate* problems and if possible be ready with alternatives. "You don't get anywhere without planning and (when problems arise) you have to have alternative plans."

Yet another shift centers on the learning system. Formal learning can teach you technical skills. Dealing with people in a task setting inevitably has to be learned informally and men have already learned the ground rules on intra-group relationships among men.

"Cooperation to get a job done—if you get swell-headed about how fast you can run then the other guys don't block for you any more." "Some people are better than others but you have to have eleven."

Still another shift in skills has to do with the formal system of relationships. The simple vertical line typical of supervision—upward to a boss, downward to subordinates—becomes complicated by a network of lateral relationships with counterparts in other areas whose input or lack of it makes an impact in terms of both budget and productivity on what your own department or group can deliver. With *no* formal authority to force a desired result, one must fall back on influence—an outcome of friendship, persuasion, favors granted and owed, promises that must be kept if you want to be operative in the future, connections with people who already *have* influence, the way you yourself are seen—are you a winner, a member of "the club," or are you a potential loser?

The experience of most little girls has no parallel. The prestigious sports for girls tend to be one on one: tennis, swimming, golf, gymnastics, skating. And in the one-on-one sports, the old adage that "it's not whether you won or lost but *how* you played the game" has been so stressed that many women tennis players now in their twenties still play for "exercise"—they don't play to win. While this is changing, it is changing slowly. There cannot be many fathers with the courage to face the ridicule that must have attached to the brave man who fought the sneering insistence of the Little League coach that his daughter wear a protective cup in order to qualify for the baseball team.

Team sports. One team against another. Aiming to win, to reach an objective. It means one must develop a strategy that takes the environment into account. Who and what can help? Who and what can hinder?

When? How much? How do I make use of this or counter that in order to get where I want to go? And if the objective is career advancement through the management ranks of today's corporation, who is most likely to win—the man who sees that world as it is, a world of winning and losing, of teams, of stars, of average and mediocre players, in essence *his* world, or the woman struggling to find a world as it should be, as it ought to be, in search of the best possible method?

Before we are misunderstood we want to make very clear that we are placing no value judgment whatsoever on the aim to win. We are not saying it is either good or bad. What we are saying is that it is real, very real, and that far more men feel, see and act on that reality than do women. Strategy now has a bad sound, a legacy of politicians who lost sight of moral objectives and adopted without question both the tenuous ethics of the game plan and a language drawn intact from the football field; men who took the concept of winning and made it an end in itself, never questioning the meaning of what they won since winning was enough in itself. We would guess, and it is a guess, that very few women indeed could develop a mind-set of this kind because so few women think of winning in personal terms. If anything, women tend to exemplify the other extreme—"Do the best you can and hope someone will notice you." For both men and women the answer to this dilemma of extremes probably lies somewhere in the middle ground—and if men need to lessen the drive to win, women as certainly need to develop it.

This does not mean that women should become more like men. It does mean that women as thinking people should assess much more concretely what's in it for them—what it is they really want, how to go about getting it and what the costs and rewards of getting it will be. If women begin to ask these questions, they must of necessity take the environment into consideration.

Yet another pattern of difference lies in the way men and women see risk. What is risk? What does it mean? The difference in response is striking. Men see risk as loss or gain; winning or losing; danger or opportunity. The responses in every group we have taught have balanced in this way—one man responds negatively, another responds postively, and they both agree that these are the two faces of risk.

Women see risk as entirely negative. It is loss, danger, injury, ruin, hurt. One avoids it as best one can. And there is yet another dimension: men see risk as affecting the future; it is risking one's potential, risking future gain, risking career advancement. A bad mistake and you may never move again. Women see risk as affecting the here and now, what they have so far managed to achieve, all that they have. One woman captured this issue in its entirety when she told us, "My husband always says to me, 'Shoot for the moon and the worst you can do is fall on a star!' And I've just realized that every time he says it I always respond, 'Sure you will. On one of the points.' "

One has only to ask oneself what this means to begin to see the behavioral answers. Risk perceived as a here-and-now danger to what one has discounts future danger; if none is perceived in the present, none is assumed in the future. For example, a recently promoted woman, a divisional product manager in an old, established consumer goods company, told us that she simply could not understand how her new boss could tolerate one of her counterparts, an incompetent fifty-seven-year-old man, his senior in age, his junior in rank and a smooth-feathered winger if ever there was one. She thought her boss was extremely competent, she liked him and she respected him, except for this.

"This guy has an even larger office than my boss. He comes in at ten o'clock and he goes to the health club at three. If you heard him in a meeting you wouldn't know he was talking about the same products. And nobody says anything!" No, she admitted, no one took him very seriously either but that wasn't the point —why was he even there? If it were up to her she would fire him, retire him early, do something, anything, but get him out of there. She felt even more strongly about it when a bright new employee whom she had interviewed for her department was hired away by his. She went to her boss. But, she said, "He laughed it off. Oh, he said things like, 'Good old Joe. You've got to get to know him. He's been here much longer than I have. He knows his way around.' Sure he knows his way around. To all the best restaurants. He does nothing all day and now they've let him have one of the brightest people we hired this year. Someone I really wanted."

We knew her boss well. He was, as she said, an extremely competent manager. A few weeks later we asked him whether things had improved. He shook his head. "She's killing herself. Joe's been around a long time. He knows a lot of people and he's beginning to hear what she's saying. She doesn't see the risk. She's going to kill herself." Why didn't he sit her down and tell her that? He looked at us. "How can I tell her that Joe is where he is because the guy he went to school with, went to college with, shares a vacation house with, and as far as I know may call every night, is marketing vice-president, corporate. She's so hell-bent on what is honest, true, right and good that all it would take is for me to say, 'You're right. He's a loser. He's only here because he's got friends,' and it would be all over the division that I said it. I can't risk that. She's got to learn. I can't help thinking that somehow a man would have picked it up. Somehow a man would have figured that somewhere Joe must have friends to have survived so long. Or at least a man might ask himself, 'Who's he? How come?' and go slowly until he found out. He wouldn't come on like a crusader because that way nobody tells you anything. I can't justify Joe to a crusader. Why should I? I want a marketing career in this company, not a cause.

"And you know, Joe has his uses. When I want to get something to corporate without making a big thing of it—a new idea and I want to see if it'll fly—I give it to Joe and let him run. Every now and again it works. To the guy up there it looks as if good old Joe thinks sometimes and is worth the protection effort—and I get my suggestions in. Sure Joe's people do all his work. And I've got to be sure they're good. Joe will go in another five years. I've got twenty more years in this company."

Risk. For this man it was out there in the future, a risk to his potential for advancement, a risk recognized and the potential for loss to the best of his ability turned to advantage. She never even saw the career risk she was apparently so deliberately incurring. There was no risk to her current job involved, she couldn't be fired for the way she felt about Joe, so to her risk was really an irrelevant issue. And the irony was that no one was willing to accept the risk which changing her point of view involved.

Risk. A difference in response because of a difference in perception and a difference in behavior as a consequence of both. Again we are not attempting value judgments. We are not trying to identify what is right or what is wrong. We are simply saying—this is the way it happens and what happens is inevitably the reality with which one has to deal. Women see risk differently from the way men see it. As a result they act or don't act in terms of their own perception. Only the individual woman having recognized the difference can decide whether it is worth it to her to change.

There is one last pattern of difference and it has to do with style and with the role one must fill in a given setting. It is an elusive, shifting question. Different people to be dealt with, different tasks to be accomplished, require different roles and demand different styles. The role of subordinate is a universal one but it can be filled using one of a variety of behavioral styles. For example, the helper and the follower. With the helper one has a sense of someone who is active, who tries to assist, who uses his or her initiative; with the follower one has a sense of passivity, of someone who follows rules and obeys orders. But one might fill the role of subordinate equally well in the style of a junior colleague, or even of an equal or a friend.

How does one choose? What is decisive in determining the style to be adopted in a subordinate's role? Men's responses to these questions center on their bosses' expectations of them, women's on their own concept of themselves. It is a critical difference. It means that men will necessarily be more alert to cues and signals which women may neither hear nor see. And these signals may have to do with very small things—how one speaks and the language one uses, how one dresses, whether one appears quick and clever, or slow and reflective, whether one is a helper, or indeed a follower—and most important, when, and in front of whom and over what kinds of issues. The underlying question for most men is clear: what does this boss want, because the chances are he can make or break me for the next job.

Certainly there are men who resent, laugh at and

even refuse to adopt the style their bosses may demand. But if they do so they either sense the price they may have to pay or they have a counterstrategy—a godfather higher up in the organization, or a clearly visible talent which will advance them in any case, or a boss who in their eyes lacks the influence to block them. In one company we know of the style demanded of junior executives is that of a loyal soldier and it is precise down to the details of the uniform—Gucci shoes. The men talk about them, laugh at them. But they buy them and wear them.

Women's responses, centering as they do on who one is, place much less weight on others' demands and expectations: "This is who I am—like it or leave it." And this means that distancing oneself from the boss, the job, the situation that may have arisen, is inevitably more difficult. There is no sense of a game being played, of a temporary adoption of a different style for reasons of self-interest. It is all for real. The investment in oneself is specific, the vulnerability to criticism and to personal hurt is consequentially greater and the ability to believe that one can do a job one does not already know, or has never done before, is that much less.

How and when does the greater flexibility that men apparently have, their larger capacity for dissembling, in the value-free sense of veiling feeling, begin to develop? We heard at least part of the answer from a twenty-eight-year-old woman, a junior officer in a large eastern bank. "There was something that used to bother me. I can remember when I was about ten, my brother was two years older, and he used to play on Saturdays with a gang of boys down the street. He'd come in for lunch and we would hear every single Saturday about two of these boys. They were just terrible. He couldn't stand them. But he'd be back out playing with them after lunch. Then at dinner we'd hear it all over again. It got so impossible that I couldn't stand it and one day I said, 'If you don't like them why do you play with them?' He just stared at me and then he said, 'You've got to be crazy! We need eleven for the team!' I thought about it a lot and I simply couldn't understand it. I knew that if I felt like that about another girl there was no way I would have played with her."

What boys learn that girls don't: flexibility, how to develop a style, a way of behaving that makes it simpler to get what one wants. And most critical of all, how to develop that style among one's peers without even knowing that one is doing it—a far different thing from consciously attempting to win over authority figures like parents on a one-on-one basis. Boys learn how to put up with each other, to tolerate each other and to use each other to a degree that girls hardly ever find necessary. Later, against a background of shared assumptions and prior experience, men learn to sit at meetings and to put up with each other, to tolerate each other and to use each other to a degree that women often find incomprehensible. For men, friendship may be a valued outcome of interaction on the job. For women it too often tends to be a prerequisite.

Group behavior among men is in fact an issue women often raise: "How can two men who dislike each other intensely sit at a meeting pretending to be considerate and helpful to each other while everyone else knows what the situation is and still pretends to buy it? How can they be such hypocrites?"

It is a revealing question. Corporate manners tend to be the manners of a society whose members are bent on winning at one extreme and on sheer survival at the other, and one's position in relation to either extreme tends to define the status of one's membership. Until one has won, discretion is advisable. Why make enemies deliberately when making friends is a means of one's end? At the age of twelve, little boys already know that they need ten others to make a team and that they may or may not like them all.

The manners women bring with them are those of another society, a society whose members are bent on the maintenance of relationships for they are the most immediate definition of who one is. Relationships for women tend to be ends in themselves and there is little in the traditional feminine experience to contradict this. As a result, and without even knowing it, women tend to fall into the great trap of "overemotionalism": intolerance—"I don't like him or her and I can't work with either of them"—or a painful vulnerability to criticism.

If a woman assumes without thinking that the quality of relationships is her most important priority and acts on it, if she tends not to have tangible career objectives, if as a consequence she focuses her energies on job performance in the here and now, oblivious to the informal pressures and counterpressures that influence promotion, the chances are painfully small that she will be able to distance herself from the difficulties of the corporate present by making them current costs of a career future. The chances are not much greater that others, men, will even see her as acting as if she wanted one.

All of these differences in mind-set in fact add up to an image—an image that many women in management positions unconsciously convey to the men they work with. Men in management positions tend to judge other men on the basis of the assumptions they hold about themselves, about management careers in general and about the particular companies for which they work. Women's assumptions tend to be different on every level but this is hardly ever an issue that either men or women consciously deal with, and even the man who prides himself on being fair—"I try to treat everyone alike"—is inevitably applying the same standards he uses to evaluate himself and other men to the evaluation of women. As a result he tends to see someone who seems more diffident about getting ahead, someone he therefore assumes to be less "motivated," someone who may appear to be intolerant or overreactive in comparison with the men he supervises, someone who seems to ignore the informal side of organizations. All of these perceptions come together to the lasting disadvantage of many women as middle management positions draw near.

3

The Middle Management
Career Path

Middle management positions are often inaccurately defined on the basis of salary, fringe benefits or status —office size, a rug on the floor. They are almost never defined in terms of the actual on-the-job changes which accompany what is essentially a shift from supervisory management to broader, across-department responsibilities.

This shift is critical for both men and women and it needs to be looked at in two ways: from the standpoint of the "normal" career path leading up to it and from the point of view of a man and a woman moving toward it.

First the "normal" career path. The typical management career path moves individuals from an initial experience in a technical or specialist's role to the more general role of a middle manager. From that point career paths lead upward to new levels of specialization which demand a broader and more conceptual approach to decision-making and problem-solving.

In terms of progressive job functions, the specialist's job is essentially one of applying particular kinds of technical knowledge and experience to the solution of primarily routine problems so as to ensure the completion of assigned tasks. Supervisory responsibilities at this level are closely related to task completion and to the proper use of techniques and skills.

The middle manager's job in contrast is much more one of coordination with counterparts in other functional areas to see that the work of his or her own group or department is related as effectively as possible to the immediate objectives and operations of the enterprise; and it is primarily for this much broader task that he or she is held responsible.

At a higher level more senior managers are much less involved in seeing that work is actually done, or in meeting the day-to-day requirements of operational interdependence between and among functional areas. They are much more closely involved in setting long-term directions and developing policies for entire functional areas in order to give coherence to the operations of the enterprise as a whole.

Looked at in this way, career paths leading ultimately to the most senior levels of management inevitably and critically depend on that first important transition from technical or specialist supervision to the broader and much less precise role of a middle manager.

The transition itself demands an ability to deal competently with the following shifts in responsibility, which bear repeating, among others that are more specific to the new job function:

Transition from Supervision to Middle Management

TECHNICAL EXPERTISE:	Mastery of a specific function or area	Working knowledge of requirements of other functions/areas

GOAL-SETTING:	Meeting goals set by superiors. Short-term	Breaking down broader and longer-term inter-departmental goals and setting subgoals for subordinates
PLANNING:	Carrying out plans already decided on	Developing plans for the achievement of objectives
PROBLEM-SOLVING:	Solving problems as they arise	Anticipating problems and preparing alternative solutions in advance
INTERDEPARTMENT LIAISON:	Usually not critical to job performance	Invariably of critical importance to job performance
LEARNING BASE:	Formal and technically oriented: classes, courses, manuals, texts	Informal and behaviorally oriented: learning from others—peers, superiors and subordinates
THE INFORMAL SYSTEM:	Incidental to getting the job done	Critical to getting the job done
SELF-RELIANCE VS. RELIANCE ON OTHERS:	Where necessary, performance requirements can be met by relying on one's own skills	Must depend increasingly on the ability to delegate task performance to others

This list is not meant to be exclusive but rather to highlight the critical changes which the transition to middle management demands. It is a transition which is difficult because the emphasis on formal ways of learning the job, doing the job and moving up in the job shifts to a much more informal base.

For the woman who enters an organization with aspirations that differ significantly from a man's aspirations, who finds it difficult to say with the same emphasis, "I'm going to work for the rest of my life and I want a career," who in fact concentrates on the acquisition of competence in whatever may be her current job, leaving career advancement largely to take care of itself, the transition is supremely difficult.

If we try to follow her from her first day of work to a position ten or twelve years into the future, she tends to share a number of the characteristics of the hypothetical woman we are about to describe. Typically this woman graduates with a liberal arts degree. She has done well in languages, literature, history, psychology or sociology, music or art. She leaves college not at all sure what a skill is, with a sinking feeling that whatever it is she hasn't got it. Many women like her go to a secretarial school to acquire something they can tell themselves *is* a skill because there is a demand for it, it is tangible, it can be used. She does so too but she is lucky enough to find a job as an administrative assistant in a staff department. She types for herself but not for others. Slowly she finds her feet and begins to realize that there *are* skills that she can learn, and she can learn them on the job. As she becomes more competent her sense of security increases. She *can* learn those skills, she *can* use them effectively. As time passes she finds that their effective use contributes to her sense of security in another way. The men with whom she works begin to see her as someone who, in spite of the fact that she's a woman, is extremely good at her job. In a real way she begins to develop a sense of legitimacy, of having a right to do the job she does, both in her own mind and, as she sees their reactions, in the minds of others.

Throughout this process she tends to have made no long-term career commitment. Her commitment has been to current performance and to on-the-job competence. She is not sure for how long she will work or whether she will work at all if she gets married. Given the lack of a longer-range objective, her concentration on the here and now is understandable. She wants to make the present as worthwhile as she can. She signs up for courses that add to her expertise. She reads manuals and professional journals.

Several years later her competence earns her a supervisory position. At that point she has invested a great deal in the skills she has acquired and they in turn have contributed heavily to her sense of who she is. It is difficult for her to accept that other people, those she now supervises, will make the same investment, and in reality a number of them don't. Her way of coping with this is to pick up the pieces for them, to do the extra work herself. She becomes a true working supervisor. She is responsible for all of her old assignments, the supervision of subordinates and the added work involved in ensuring that nothing leaves her small department unless it is perfect. To ensure this she often prefers to do the job herself. Her supervisory style is a close one, she is a scrupulous checker, a dotter of *i*'s and a crosser of *t*'s.

It is not a style which breeds initiative nor does it lend itself to delegating responsibility. She sends a very clear message—she trusts and relies on herself alone. Her friends tends to be from outside of the organization and her contacts within it tend to be formal and task-oriented. If she remains in this position until her early thirties the chances are that she will decide she has a career, or at the very least that she will continue to work over the long-term. The problem is that her style has now been formed. It is a close, non-delegative style, heavily dependent on self for performance and on formal structure and rules to define both job and performance.

This style was not formed consciously, she never thought about it in terms of whether it was helpful in advancing her position or not. Bosses came and went. Depending on how competent they were, she had often to do part of their job as well. They rated her an "outstanding supervisor," aware that if she left they would probably have had to replace her with at least two people. At the same time they rated her as "probably terminal in present position." The style she developed and never thought of changing stamped "lacking in management potential" all over her, and this at a point when possibly for the first time she began to think seriously of a long-term career. Yet why should she have thought of changing her behavior? For what reason? Superiors praised the scrupulous accuracy of the work she was responsible for. Raises were forth-coming. She wasn't looking ahead to anything specific. Getting the job done competently had often been more than enough to cope with.

For many, many women this is the extraordinarily painful dilemma of the transition to middle management. The style they develop in order to survive along the path to middle management, both psychologically and tactically, is a style that makes them the fabled outstanding supervisor. But it lacks a strategic dimension, a long-term objective. As a consequence they fail to build flexibility into it, they do not measure present cost against future benefit. They do not recognize the cues that signal a need for a change in style. They concentrate on task, skill and job performance and ignore the critically important behavioral variables.

Our hypothetical woman tends to arrive at the transition point to middle management an in-depth specialist and a close supervisor of other specialists. Yet she is a woman in her mid-thirties with another thirty years ahead of her. She is bright and she is competent.

For men behavior *is* a variable along the path to middle management, their own behavior and the behavior of others. However implicit, however unconscious, the assumption that they will have to work for most of their lives gives men an objective: to make the best of it that they can—which is widely interpreted as career advancement. Typically a man comes to his first management job not even conscious of the psychological preparation for it that he has undergone since he was a small boy. Typically too his high school and college years have given him mathematical skills or a background in economics or business, together with a clear recognition of competitive striving as an inherent factor in achievement.

To him, his first job is the beginning of an apprenticeship. His expectation that once he has mastered it he will move on is a comparatively modest expectation, for countless men have done it before him. Why not he? The central issue really lies in finding the most effective way, and while his judgment of what is effective may be good or poor, at a minimum he will try.

If he is a college graduate recruited into a fast track training program he is given considerable visibility as he moves about the company. If he enters a small department in finance or marketing, or if he is hired as an assistant foreman in a manufacturing plant, his environment is considerably more limited, but his assumption that he is not going to be there for the rest of his life determines his behavior.

Learn and move on. Act so that people will see you as having the ability to move on. Try to influence the people who can help you move on. Be needed by those people, become necessary to them. Try to identify what they want and don't want. Broaden your information base from what you need to do the job to include the people who can help you leave it. Who are they—good, bad, indifferent? On whom should you focus your efforts? Find out—and try to make sure you don't pick a loser. Do job changes make sense at this point—do they promise more, more quickly? Transfers, moves to other companies? Find out—and try to pick a winner whichever way you go, a winner who can become a godfather, a rabbi, a sponsor, a patron—who will invest in you, help you, teach you and speak up for you. If you're right you'll move with him. If you're wrong—disengage and try to leave him behind. But find another.

It would be fascinating to pursue the psychoanalytic implications of this pattern. It is a pattern which repeats the search for a father, ultimate revolt and then finally the drive to become a father oneself. It is a pattern drawn from a boy's earliest experience, with the father representing power, authority and freedom to take on the entire world. It is a pattern still basic to this society's definition of the male identity and it is the common heritage of men who manage. It is the way their world works.

It is against this background that our hypothetical young man reaches the middle management transition point. He reaches it more quickly and far more economically than the hypothetical young woman whose path we followed. When he gets there, what he did along the way tends to have given him a much broader knowledge and understanding of how the organization functions—of its purposes and its people, particularly those who matter to him. Like her he has more often than not had to master a particular technical area,* but his investment in it has not been as deep because the pressures on him were different. In her case over-investment gave her legitimacy and thus security in her eyes and in the eyes of others. In his case he brought legitimacy with him and saw his security as resting on quite different foundations: in being seen by the men who mattered as a young man with "potential."

At the transition point her great fear is to be cut off from what she knows, from the comforting familiarity of an area she has mastered in depth, from the very basis of her sense of legitimacy and security, only to confront new and quite different problems, new and quite different people, in a setting where she may now be the *only* woman in such a position.

His great fear is that he may be entering a back-water, cut off from the people who helped him. Can he put a team together? Will he find capable subordinates? What will his peers be like? Will his new boss be a man from whom he can learn—who has influence enough to help him advance?

Her perception of the problems facing her is centered on herself, on her own capacity or lack of it. It is an inward preoccupation which dulls her ability to assess other people objectively. She tends to see them

---

* However, we know of a number of cases, and there must be others, where men *began* their careers as assistants to the president, developed a basic knowledge of the function of a number of departments but no special expertise in any, came to be seen as true "generalists," stayed at the top with title changes designating more and more over-all responsibility and skipped the middle management bind completely.

in terms of the impact they have on her own sense of adequacy.

His perception of the problems facing him is centered on the people around him, on *their* abilities. It is an outward preoccupation which sharpens his awareness of who those people are and what they want—and the one tends to condition whether he will give them the other.

Her problems feed upon each other. Where before, her expertise was proof of her right to be where she was, she feels she must prove that right all over again both to herself and to the men around her. And she must do it at a more complex level of responsibility, at a time when she is supremely conscious that she lacks mastery of the job she must do.

Driven by the old anxiety over legitimacy—the need to justify to herself and others that in spite of the fact she's a woman she knows the job and can handle it—and with few examples of other women who have ever done it to give her confidence, she retreats into herself. She avoids asking questions for fear they might indicate ignorance of the aspects of the job she feels she *should* know. This blocks her ability to learn. Anxiety invests every gap in knowledge and experience with the same importance and she drives herself to work on her own time at understanding every detail—relevant or not—while she copes, as she must, with the day-to-day pressures of the job. The apparent confidence and self-assuredness of the men around her, however unreal, make her situation seem even worse.

A third-level manager in a Bell System company gave us a description of this painful process a year after her promotion to district management.†

† In most Bell companies there are only seven levels of management, from first management job to president. Third or district level is the first true middle management level as we have defined it.

"I was promoted after the Consent Decree.‡ All of the companies had to promote a certain number of women and I guess I was one of them. I think I deserved the promotion but I sometimes wonder whether I would have gotten it without the decree.

"I came out of the Traffic Department. This is where all the operators are and it's really a women's department. Men used to come into it as management trainees. The women trained them. And then the men managed *us*—sometimes the very same men we'd trained.

"I came up the operators' route all the way to group chief and then chief operator. My promotion to district manager (third level) was one of the first for women.

"I'll never forget what those early months were like. I really had no management experience. I only knew vaguely what the other departments were responsible for and I didn't know whom to ask or what to ask. The worst thing was wondering whether my counterparts—who were all men—believed I'd got the job simply because of EEOC. I know some of them did, and at the beginning I couldn't even make myself ask a question in case it turned out to be a question I should have known the answer to. I was really afraid to have that happen. I could hear their minds clicking: 'Third level and doesn't even know the job.'

‡ On January 18, 1973, American Telephone & Telegraph representing its twenty-two subsidiary companies entered into a landmark settlement with the Department of Labor and the Equal Employment Opportunity Commission. Under the terms of a Consent Decree, AT&T agreed to pay $15 million in restitution to an estimated fifteen thousand women and minorities who had allegedly been discriminated against in job assignments, pay and promotions; another $23 million a year in pay raises; and to establish goals and timetables for the hiring and promotion of women and minorities into its management ranks. In return, the EEOC and the Department of Labor agreed to withdraw the various charges leveled against the corporation. AT&T is the nation's largest private employer.

"My first district meeting was a total disaster. There I was, the only woman, a district manager, Traffic. There they were. They knew each other. Most of them had years of district experience. They came from the tough departments where there were *no* women— Plant, Network, Engineering, as well as the others.

"Most of the meeting went straight over my head. They got into a very technical discussion at one point. I didn't know what most of the equipment was or what it was supposed to do. I didn't know the technical systems definitions and they didn't bother to spell them out. They used letters. E.S.S. is a simple one— Electronic Switching Systems.

"By the end of the meeting I had a column of letters and I spent night after night with the manuals trying to figure them out. I didn't dare ask anyone. It sounds silly now—but it wasn't then. I nearly quit. If it hadn't been for my husband I *would* have quit. I remember one set of letters that nearly finished me. P.O.T.S. I looked it up in every manual. I went through literally hundreds of pages trying to find a reference. I finally got to know one of the district guys and a couple of months later I asked him. He laughed. He said it meant 'Plain Old Telephone Service.' "

It is difficult to forget that woman, the anxiety she felt and the obsessive way in which she tried to deal with it. Anxiety of the same kind drives the younger woman in search of psychological security and organizational legitimacy to overinvestment in specialization. When she finds it, the seal that reads "Yes, you belong. Yes, you have a right to be here. Yes, in spite of the fact that you're a woman, you *can* do this job" is a tough one to give up.

When it is given up at the middle management transition point the risks begin all over again and the psychological stakes are higher. The security of solid technical competence in a specific area is no longer enough. One can no longer rely on and trust oneself alone. The learning system changes, the system of implementation changes, and *in the nature of the relationships that men traditionally establish with each other lies the key to both*. Godfathers look after godsons.

For women who were daughters, not sons, such relationships are laden with difficulty. If they exist at all they are usually seen as heavily burdened with sexual overtones, or if not, as so asexual that the woman involved is described as "masculine," "a hard, tough bitch who's good at the job and nothing else."

Most women want neither and avoid both. Yet the trap is formidable: at one level, because you're a woman you feel you *must* know the job to justify even being there; at another level, because you're a woman there are far greater risks attached to developing the relationships which help you learn; and at still another deeper level, because you're a woman "femininity" and its relationship to your sense of who you are, are painfully manipulable variables.

The Bell System manager who said "If it hadn't been for my husband I would have quit" was almost certainly addressing this last issue. Whatever she faced as a woman on the job, her husband reinforced her as a person who was a woman and who could hold that job. Single women are far more vulnerable.

Given all of this, is there any answer? If there is, does it help women or does it merely certify that the difficulties are real?

We think that there is an answer, and that it does both. In acknowledging the difficulties, in explaining why they exist, it gives women a perspective of central importance. Women who thought that individually and alone they were the singular source of the problems they faced in "masculine" jobs, careers, roles and settings can see that to one degree or another all women share these problems because a common heritage of beliefs and assumptions shapes our concept of ourselves. If we are ever to change those that cripple our ability to achieve, then it is critically important to understand how and why they came to exist— beginning at the very beginning with the concept of femininity and the ways in which its formation differs from the psychological development of men.

4

Growing Up
Male or Female

Men and women alike take from the structure of their family relationships a basic sense of their own identity and an equally basic model for the relationships they later develop with others. In a culture dominated by the nuclear family, as ours is, the first and most important relationship that a child of either sex develops is with its mother and the dynamics of this relationship are the same for both boys and girls. Children of both sexes love, want and depend on their mother. Their sense of identity is inextricably tied to her. She confirms that they exist in their own eyes for good or for bad.

The Oedipus complex, as Freudian theory developed it, is concerned with the emotional trauma the little boy undergoes in finally coming to terms with the need to break away from his mother. At the age of three or four, little boys often say with the most appealing naïveté and sometimes with real passion—that they are going to marry their mother when they grow up. The painful resolution of this issue, the little boy's acceptance that he cannot, has been described in detail in the literature and has been summarized only recently as "a colossal failure,"[1] a failure which the small boy copes with by deferring childhood's love and desire.

The fact is that a little boy gives up his first attachment to his mother, *under whatever real or imagined threat,* essentially to wait for another woman in adolescence and adulthood. The sense of loss, the damage done to the psychological self, to the fragile sense of self-esteem, the sense of abandonment have all been movingly reported in clinical research. These are issues which are painfully difficult to deal with but the child must deal with them, and he does so in several ways: by attempts at repression which seek to drive the awareness of loss and pain from consciousness; by attempts at denial which seek to assert that neither loss nor pain exists; by externalization of the aggression that results from injury to the sense of self—in a destructive way against others and objects, or in a constructive way through activities which develop skill, knowledge and experience; or by internalizing aggression, directing it against the self and holding the self to be worthless and deserving of the injury.

The probability is that none of these attempts at coping with psychological injury succeeds on its own. They work in combination and the relative emphasis given to one over the other will depend heavily on the support which the environment provides or fails to provide in the attitudes and expectations of important others. The important others are of course pre-eminently the parents, but because the crisis occurs at an age (between five and seven) when the little boy is typically beginning school, making friends of other little boys and developing his first interests outside of the family, these developments provide additional and important sources of support. The little boy is now at an age to take part in masculine activities and his father's interest in and attention to him typically increase. He is expected to be aggressive and he is rewarded for it by both parents and peers. He is expected to run himself ragged at games, to be independent, to initiate. He is, in short, rewarded and confirmed for deflecting aggression into useful paths and he begins to acquire a sense of confidence in his own ability progressively to master his small environment.

Whatever the defensive emphasis the little boy might have tended to choose, the pressures of socialization make two routes clear: first, the externalization of aggression in constructive ways; and second, denial.

The constructive use of aggression is rewarding in itself and it is rewarded for itself. It helps confirm the child's basic sense of who he is in the eyes of others at a time when the emotional trauma of the Oedipal resolution places that sense in jeopardy. In the active company of his small peers, girls come to be regarded as inferior, second-rate, weaker and more timid than boys. This is a development based as much on a realistic assessment of society's traditional view of girls as on the unconscious need it is made to serve of denying the pain of the "colossal failure" associated with the Oedipal resolution.

The loss of the first attachment to the mother, a woman, is denied by a primitive acceptance that women, "girls," are not worth being attached to. At a conscious level, an exception is made for the mother especially if she reinforces the assumption of male superiority in her preference for a son. She is "special" so long as he is "special." At an unconscious level the trauma of losing her and thus of losing part of the boy's identity evokes the need for repression, of pain, denial of rejection, and aggressive self-expression. It is not for nothing that boys at this age mercilessly taunt others who still remain close to their mothers. The "sissies" represent a threat that is still painfully close to the surface.

The pervasiveness of this individual pattern of loss, of defenses which seek to deal with it essentially by finding compensations which mesh with attempts at denial, and of a social structure of beliefs and assumptions which provide both compansation and a rationale for denial can be detected from seeming triva. Not long ago (1973), a television sports documentary showed two brothers who were champion horseshoe throwers. The elder, who seemed to be thirteen or fourteen, had just been beaten by the younger, who seemed to be about eleven. The younger boy disarmingly told the interviewer that his victory was not entirely deserved because his older brother had competed with a sprained finger. How did that happen? "Well," said the younger brother cheerfully, "I called him a girl and he went after me."

At a much later point in age and experience, James Lovell, Jr., one of the astronaut heroes, made this hardly surprising statement: "We have not sent any women into space because we have not had a good reason to. We fully envision, however, that in the near future we will fly women into space and use them in the same way we use them on earth—and for the same purpose."[2]

In every sense the little boy's way out of the emotional trauma which generations of psychoanalysts have studied and recorded with inexhaustible sympathy is structured for him. There is the openly encouraged distraction into activity and the rewards which confirm the little boy's sense of who he is; there is society's confirmation of his own attempts at denial of loss—he has not lost because what he had lost, the feminine side of his identity, was hardly worth keeping; and there is the added compensation that in society's view as a man he is inherently superior to half the human race, or at the very least at this point in time, to half the human beings of *his* race.

All of these issues combine to leave him sometimes fiercely, and more often fearfully, opposed to any changes in the structure of social beliefs and assumptions, customs and traditions which might affect his role as a man, and thus his concept of masculinity, and thus his sense of identity—each of which has been established, in reverse order, on the basis of psychological defenses which those same social beliefs and assumptions, customs and traditions have selectively emphasized.

It is at this point that we need to ask, clearly, unequivocally and insistently: *What happens to the little girl?* She starts out with the same emotional ties. Her tie to her mother is as real and as profound as is her brother's. She too loves, wants and depends on her mother. Her sense of identity is linked as inextricably to her mother. Where is there any account of the trauma she endures? There is none, and in its place a massive contradiction has developed. Having conceded that the little girl must necessarily share the little boy's attachment to his mother, psychoanalytic theory then discounts the reality of the emotions which the little girl must deal with as she grows older even as it places overwhelming emphasis on the emotional reality for the little boy.

The little girl is assumed to be capable of switching her emotional allegiance—an allegiance which is theoretically held to be supremely difficult for the boy to break—in the blink of an eye. She is in theory supposed to recognize that because she lacks a penis she is, therefore, a mutilated boy; she is assumed to realize that her mother also lacks a penis and has, therefore, passed the mutilation on to her; her self-hatred at her own mutilation and her rejection of her mutilated mother are then held to be the catalysts which allow her to transfer her affection to her father, who is the possessor of the longed-for penis. By virtue of yet another leap in the imaginative dark her desire for the penis then becomes a desire for its product, a child, and only then is she believed to have finally accepted her mutilation and to be on the road to developing the passivity which is fitting and proper for adult womanhood.

What happens in reality? The tradition which holds that boys are more desirable than girls often makes a mother appear to be less emotionally involved with a small daughter than she is with a son. The mother, conditioned by the very tradition she now invokes against her daughter, tends to give the little girl an endless stream of clues of the child's second place in the order of things. By the age of four or five when little boys are blithely saying that they are going to marry their mother when they grow up, little girls are already aware that for them such a *mésalliance* is particularly out of the question. How do little girls cope with this? For boys it is a "colossal failure." What is it for girls? For boys it is a deferment of childhood's love and desire, an extension of the pattern. Ultimately they will regain what they have lost. For girls it is a radical change in the pattern itself, a greater complexity, whose resolution they must take on trust, for what was lost cannot be regained. How does a little girl cope with this? How does she cope with the sense of loss and abandonment, with the damage done to the psychological self, to the fragile sense of self-esteem? How does she cope with the uncertainty over the meaning of relationships which develops out of the pattern set by the dissolution of this first relationship? Where are the emotional supports, the socially sanctioned superiority which allow for denial of loss, the distractions made available to little boys as *they* emerge out of the Oedipal crisis—a crisis in which their fundamentally important first relationship with another human being becomes a "colossal failure"? How can the little girl work through the aggression which erupts from psychological injury? Is a little girl rewarded and confirmed for being outwardly aggressive? Is she encouraged to run herself ragged at games, to be independent, to be an initiator, to learn how things work—in effect, to deflect aggression away from herself to mastering her own small environment?

If she is very lucky she is—and her father often does much of it for her. If she is less lucky she tries on her own and simmers with rebellion in the face of criticism by others that she is a tomboy, unladylike, not "a nice little girl." If she is simply the average little girl she tends to give up. The pain associated with the loss of the mother-daughter relationship is dealt with by repression, and at a conscious level, by accepting one's role and place as deserved. As a girl one is necessarily less than a boy. Inadequate in many things. Unable to do as many more.

In adolescence the reawakening of sexuality brings with it a reawakening of the fear, the resentment, and sometimes the hatred, associated with the much earlier attempt to cope with the loss of the first relationship to the mother. It is not a "last battle for masculinity" as Helene Deutsch claimed. It is too often a last battle for identity in the truest sense of seeking relationships which by their depth and strength can define who one is and affirm what one can do, what one is worth, given that the very first relationship, which set the prototypical pattern for the development of others, was broken amid pressures which set rigid limits on the growth of an identity rooted in what one *could* do, what one *was* worth—which in essence pressed the child into a role that allowed for far less self-expression than was encouraged in her brother.

Certainly no one copes with issues of this kind at a conscious level. They may be repressed or they may be denied, coming to consciousness in fantasies and dreams in which roles are often satisfyingly reversed. For the girls repression may well be the fundamental coping mechanism. The facilitating mechanism of denial—the ability to say it isn't so, it isn't my fault—an ability which helps immeasurably to preserve one's sense of self-esteem and which the emotional dynamics within the family and the structured societal preference for boys both combine to give their brothers—is one they must acquire, if they can, on their own.

In an important summary and discussion of research on the psychology of sex differences, Maccoby and Jacklin[3] illustrate most of these issues and their work provides still further insight into the differences in perception between men and women in management careers which we have already discussed. While they note how little has been done to relate differences in self-concepts between boys and girls to the formation of ego defenses, they cite research findings which make strikingly clear how close the relationship in fact is. Boys, for example, score higher than girls on "lie" and "defensiveness" scales which are designed to assess the degree to which individuals avoid self-evaluation and instead present themselves in a favorable light.[4] Boys do not reveal thoughts and feelings to parents or peers as readily as girls do and they defend their egos "by turning against a real or presumed external frustrating object whereas girls engage in more self-blame."[5]

Boys, in other words, engage much more readily in denial.

Boys also boast more. Between the ages of seven and eleven they engage more often in "attempting to call attention to oneself by boasting, or by performing praiseworthy or blameworthy acts with the intent of becoming the focus of attention."[6] And boys believe much more in their ability to control their own fates. Society's stereotype of masculinity reinforces this belief in many forms, not the least of which is what is actually learned in school. A 1973 study of elementary school textbooks by Jacklin and Mischel found that "when good things happened to a male character in a story they were presented as resulting from his own actions. Good things happening to a female character (of which there were considerably fewer) were at the initiative of others, or simply grew out of the situation in which the girl character found herself."[7] Boys see themselves as stronger, more dominant and more powerful than girls, and consistently overestimate their own positions in a "toughness hierarchy."[8] As they grow older boys' ability to see the bright side of things expands. "Even with respect to social sensibility—a presumedly feminine trait—young men seem not to 'hear' comments to the effect that they are insensitive, and their self-ratings of sensitivity are scarcely affected by negative feedback . . . If this male selective filter operates across a fairly wide range of behaviors, it might help to explain men's greater feeling of potency."[9]

In summarizing a number of studies Maccoby and Jacklin identify a "male cluster" of findings among college students made up of "greater self-confidence when undertaking new tasks, and a greater sense of potency, *specifically* including the feeling that one is in a position to determine the outcome of sequences of events that one participates in."[10]

Side by side with these findings are others which indicate the predisposition of young men and women to use successful past experience as a prediction of success in the future. Studies of both sexes in college show that men are more likely than women to expect to do well, that they judge their own performance more favorably and that they predict future performance will be at least as good and perhaps better. Women whose grades were often better than those of their male peers were nevertheless more likely to predict that they would do less well than they had in the past.[11]

The fear, perhaps the certainty, of loss and disappointment emerges undeniably. The defense of discounting it by expecting that it will happen paralyzes one's belief in one's own abilities and inevitably shackles individual initiative. If loss or failure is seen as the outcome of one's actions it is so much simpler not to want to achieve, not to have to decide, to keep one's options endlessly open so that one never closes anything off. And this in itself has a double edge: nothing is closed off so nothing is lost; because nothing is closed off no action can be taken which might lead to loss.

Not surprisingly Maccoby and Jacklin found that one difference between girls and boys consistently borne out by research was that girls conform much more readily to the demands of authority figures—for example, parents and teachers.[12] Boys in conforming less readily are at the same time more preoccupied with struggling for dominance among themselves.

Some interesting questions arise. Are girls more compliant because they fear more? And if it is fear, don't the roots of fear for both sexes lie in the prospect of self-diminishment? Is the psychological loss of the mother the prototype for the sense of self-diminishment? Are boys far more than girls both psychologically comforted (loss is not final—what was lost will be regained in adulthood) and socially supported (the compensatory benefit is male superiority and its multiple manifestations) in their attempts to deal with this first experience of self-diminishment? As a result are boys far more than girls encouraged to build defenses which simultaneously deny the sense of self-diminishment and seek to establish a sense of control?

In their survey of the research Maccoby and Jacklin found further that boys are altogether more gregarious than girls in terms of the number of peers with whom they interact and in their dependence upon the group for a system of values and as a source of activity.[13] In childhood and adolescence, in groups and teams, boys support each other, confirming each other's place in a hierarchy of both friendship and dominance and in the search for freedom from the strictures of authority, and adult control. More independent of adult authority, they impose upon themselves a structure of values which include cooperation and competition. Much more than girls they seek a group identity which particularly in team sports provides possibilities for both real and vicarious achievement while it leaves failure more often than not to be parceled out in small and tolerable pieces.

All of these issues are outcomes of the process of socialization—the development of an individual from child to adult in a certain culture whose values selectively emphasize certain things and whose rules and procedures have been established in order to attain them.

Our value system has always emphasized male superiority, our laws have embodied it and they are only now beginning to change. People, both men and women, have accepted it, and roles, relationships and individual personalities have been structured by it. The differences in perception between the men and women in management we have studied are themselves outcomes of it. Yet the only intellectual differences that have been fairly well established are that girls on the average have greater verbal ability then boys; that boys on the average have greater visual-spatial ability; and that as a consequence of these two differences there is considerable confusion over differences in mathematical ability.[14]

At quite a different level, a third established difference has to do with the propensity to *physical* aggression which is hormonally based and is greater in boys. It would be difficult to put this particular difference in clearer perspective than do Maccoby and Jacklin: "Aggression may be the primary means by which apes and little boys dominate one another (although even here the ability to maintain alliances is important). However (physical) aggression is certainly not the method most commonly employed for leadership among mature human beings."[15]

It is in this light that the questionnaire responses, the feelings, perceptions and attitudes of the management women we have interviewed and worked with need to be both seen and understood. The overriding issues of self-esteem, the damage done to it and the inability to deny the pain which compensatory advantages allow for men emerge out of the past to become part of the unquestioned definition of "femininity" for many individual women. Felt, struggled with, fought against, it is metamorphosed into a drive for legitimacy, security, clarity, certainty and structure. Even style is fixed. Much earlier, limits were set on self-expression, roles were imposed—and the pattern repeats itself: "I can't do this because I've never done it before." Or, "I can't do this because women have never done it before." The chance of failure is seen as inordinately high—the cost of the first was enormous —and risk as a result is a negative. Aggression is turned against the self and dealt with by projection back onto an environment which is experienced as threatening and hostile. One may feel that. But perhaps it isn't so. The problem is, one feels it—and tends to act on it.

Given all of this, what do we do? Is there an answer or has the existence of difficulty simply been underlined ten times?

The answer lies where it must lie—in the recognition by individual women of the extent to which some or all of these issues affect them, and, even more important, why. This is the first step toward distancing oneself from assumptions *about oneself* that are now so old, so durable, so apparently tried and true, that they are no longer even questioned. Those assumptions grew out of a different reality, a past emotional reality whose impact created them, and one re-creates that reality to the extent that one unthinkingly assumes one must. How much does it take to be able to say: "This is how it was. This is how I felt. This is how I thought. This is how I acted. And I still do— and I never thought about it." How much does it take to anticipate that you will still feel, think and act as you have always done?—and then stop and think through the implications of doing so. You can ask a great many questions in the attempt to identify those implications. Are you clear on what you want to achieve, and why, or are you simply reacting as you have always done? Who are the people involved? How do they see you? How do they see themselves— what do *they* want out of the situation? And, possibly most important of all, what do *you* want? In the long-term as well as the short.

In Part II of this book we shall take a close look at a group of twenty-five unusual women in top management positions whose strength more than anything else lay in their ability to look at the long-term and to define what they wanted. We shall see that they came from unusual backgrounds, growing up in families whose values placed heavy stress on the ability to achieve. In following them through their lives, however, we are not attempting to set them up as models for anyone. Coming from the backgrounds they did, they went to work at an unusual time and moved into middle management during World War II, when vast numbers of men were overseas and opportunities for women increased enormously. What is of absorbing interest about them is less the over-all pattern of their lives and much more the component parts of the pattern. For women wrestling with the problems of a management career, their experience helps define organizational priorities and expectations. Unless one understands those priorities and those expectations, one cannot decide whether one will accept them, reject them, work to modify them, negotiate them or trade them off.

OUT OF DATE

PART II

5
Twenty-five Women Who Made It

In Part I we sought to identify and explain a series of critical differences in the ways in which men and women who are managers view their jobs, their careers, their organizations and the people with whom they work. We saw that men bring to the management setting a clearer, stronger and more definitive understanding of where they see themselves going, what they will have to do, how they will have to act and what they must take into account if they are to achieve the objectives they set for themselves. In contrast, we saw that women are much less likely to bring to the same setting the insights, understandings and skills which from boyhood men have acquired and developed among themselves—a mind-set learned, acculturated and socialized which gives men an immediate advantage as they move into management positions.

We saw that women bring a different mind-set with them. We looked at cultural, social and in particular psychological explanations for the differences we found and we are acutely aware that in themselves these explanations may simply serve to confirm the view that "so it is and so it was and so it always will be." One knows that there are differences. One knows at least in part why these differences exist. And one knows that because of them many more men than women will begin careers in management better prepared for the environment and much more obviously motivated to achieve. Who is to say that it could be any different, and if it could be different, how?

The rest of this book will attempt to respond to these questions. To begin, we shall take a detailed look at twenty-five women who in our own past and present have successfully held top management positions in business and industry across the United States.[1] The mind-set of assumptions and attitudes which this group of pioneering women shared is in marked contrast to the mind-sets of the women in management we discussed in Part I. One begins to see in the lives of the twenty-five clear proof of the need for far more women to consider and to deal with the issues raised in Part I—and even clearer proof that the ability to achieve the highest levels of management responsibility heavily depends on doing so.

In Part III we want to look at the future. Most women will not bring with them to adulthood the strengths of the twenty-five, nor will they want to pay the price they paid. Yet there is still a great deal that women *can* do to make themselves more effective in the management environment. Women who recognize this and act on it will inevitably affect the assumptions and attitudes of men in management and just as inevitably the beliefs and assumptions that underlie women's traditional roles in the family and society.

When Margaret Hennig completed her study of these twenty-five women the results of the 1970 United States census were not yet available. The 1960 census figures set the context in which research was begun and those figures showed that of the 1.2 million people employed in the category of Officials, Managers and Proprietors who earned $10,000 or more only 25,000 were women. Women therefore represented approximately 2 per cent of the group of people who earned at least this amount. Of these 25,000 about half were employed by retail organizations, one quarter were insurance company employees and slightly under 3,000 worked in banks. The remainder, approximately 3,500 in total, were employed in *all* other types of business.

Twenty-five women, all of whom held line positions as presidents or divisional vice-presidents of nationally recognized firms, cooperated to make the study possible. In many ways they are classic pioneers not simply in terms of their unusual accomplishments but in the difficulties they overcame and the price they paid to break open new territory not just for themselves but inevitably for all women.

In order to avoid personal bias in selecting the twenty-five, three management experts were asked to serve on an independent selection panel. These three independent judges were asked to select from lists drawn from Who's Who in American Women, the national roster of biographies of members of the National Association of Business and Professional Women, the membership of other national professional women's organizations and the listings of officers in the annual reports of the *Fortune* 500 corporations. The judges were asked to select any woman listed who in their opinion as professors of business administration met the following criteria:

1. Had a full-time, continuous work history—with her jobs appearing to be sequentially related to and part

of a developing career (with no kinship ties to the ownership of the firm or any major executive working for it).

2. Held a current position at the level of corporate vice-president or president or chief executive officer of a corporation or large divisional operation.

3. Was employed by a firm which could be characterized as a medium/large, generally recognized company in its field.

4. Held a position which appeared to represent line authority and would probably include the management of men.

5. Was not employed in a position or type of business generally considered as "feminine"*

Approximately one hundred women were identified by the panel using these criteria and all of them were contacted by mail. Some did not respond, some refused cooperation, a number had to be eliminated because of career or life changes which took them out of one or more of the categories set and a few were incorrectly chosen. Thirty-five women were finally located who were willing to cooperate and each met all of the established criteria.

Nine were corporation presidents or chief executive officers and the others were divisional vice-presidents. Of the thirty-five, twenty-five were located on the eastern seaboard and the remainder in other parts of the country. In the end it became impossible to travel beyond the East for interviewing, and the women finally selected were the group of twenty-five on the eastern seaboard.

Because of the exploratory nature of the study, no approach was made to the group of twenty-five until a pilot survey was completed. The subjects of the pilot were the ten women located off the eastern seaboard

---

* For example retailing or the cosmetics industry.

who could not be included in the group of twenty-five. They were asked to write about whatever they considered most important about themselves and their careers. They were asked what they thought had contributed most to their success, and what had created the greatest problems for them, and they were asked to respond to a first draft of a questionnaire intended for use with the twenty-five.

Successive interviews, some lasting as long as three and a half hours, were then conducted with each of the twenty-five. The interviews were open-ended but where necessary the interviewer's questions ensured that the study's major interests were fully covered. Each woman wrote and submitted an autobiographical statement and after all the interviews were completed the questionnaire was used to verify factors such as age, birth order, family background, education, exact descriptions of jobs held and rates of progression.

Later on the questionnaire was administered to three other groups of women to provide comparisons with the group of twenty-five. Not all of this comparative data was directly relevant, but it proved to support the high incidence of certain background characteristics in the twenty-five.†

The other groups questioned later were: 1) Twenty-five women similar in age who were still at the middle management level; 2) twenty-five women M.B.A. graduates of Harvard Business School; and 3) twenty-five undergraduate women in their senior year who were majoring in business administration at Simmons College.

Finally, an additional group of twenty-five women, matched as nearly as possible to the original group of twenty-five in background, education and career ex-

---

† For example, all twenty-five were first-born. Most of the women in the comparison groups were also first-born.

perience through middle management, with the difference that they had given up their careers at that point, were interviewed as to why they had done so. The purpose of these interviews was to see whether any significant differences existed between these women's childhood, college and early career experiences and those of the twenty-five. If differences did appear they might help explain why the twenty-five were able to continue their careers beyond the middle management stage.

The data compiled on the primary group of twenty-five fell into five periods: 1) childhood; 2) adolescence; 3) college; 4) the first career decade; and 5) career maturity.

The reasons for this are fairly obvious. Events occurring and experiences undergone in childhood and adolescence play an essential and enduring part in a person's mature life. For twenty-five women who assumed executive positions in what was still very much a man's world, these periods were particularly important because gender identification and role modeling primarily occur within them.

College and the first career decade were selected as time blocks on the basis of research findings which indicated that career decisions made during the college years are repeatedly questioned and tested in the early career years.[2]

The final period covering the years of career maturity was selected because the findings of the pilot survey indicated that the ten women who participated in the pilot were very different—in their concerns, their expressed self-concepts, their self-ideals and the behavioral styles they appeared to have adopted—from the middle management and Harvard M.B.A. women who were also studied. Once past the first career decade something seemed to have happened to these women which made them change drastically. What happened, why and when were questions which study of the twenty-five was to answer.

The implementation of the study was straightforward. First, the early lives of the twenty-five were analyzed in the broadest possible way. Essentially the researcher sought for things which might have happened to them in common on the assumption that commonality of early experience might help explain how they came to choose the careers they did and might have contributed to the success they achieved. This line of questioning was followed through adolescence and then the analysis moved to the period of career choice and entry. Here, the study sought to understand how and why these women came to choose a management career, what the process of choice was like and in what ways their early life experiences were related to both. It sought to understand their self-concepts, their self-ideals and finally in the career years, the behavioral styles which emerged from their perception of themselves and the roles they played.

The terms self-concept and self-ideal were used very simply: self-concept referred to the picture the person held of herself at the time, who and what she thought she was. Self-ideal referred to what she thought she would like to become, what she really hoped to become. The usefulness of a self-ideal to anyone is that it provides goals for growth and improvement. As with all ideals, these goals are no sooner approached than they tend to be expanded to higher levels of difficulty and the process of working toward them is begun anew. On the other hand, as people grow and mature they become more realistic and the ideals they set for themselves become more practical and less imbued with fantasy.

Particularly important to the definition of a woman

executive's reality is the need to cope with the cultural and social bias she faces at work, and there were two points in the careers of the twenty-five when these biases would prove critical: the point of choice and entry, and the point at which the individual woman reached her highest career level. The first is concerned with the problem of getting the job, and the second with the problem of commanding the job. The twenty-five would have had to live with and adjust to these biases throughout their careers but the incidence of bias would almost certainly have been highest at these points. The table below provides a framework for looking at the ways in which the group of twenty-five might have coped with the problems of bias they encountered.

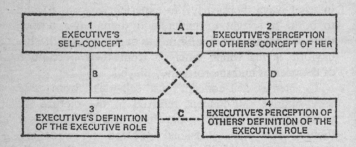

All four of these issues are interrelated, but the relationships noted as A, B, C and D are particularly important. For men, relationship A would be extremely important and incongruities in relationship B would cause difficulty for anyone. Similarly, difficulties in relationship C could pose problems for men or women in their relations with others at work. In any of these three relationships a woman might well expect to meet with approximately the same degree of apparent success and difficulty as her male counterpart. However in relationship C, the possibility of problems developing simply because she is a woman arises for the first time and these problems could become manifest in relationship D.

It is here, in the fit between others' concept of a particular woman and their concept of the executive role, that the particular woman tends to lose her individuality and to become *any* woman. Because the executive role is seen by many people (men and women) as an exclusively male role, no matter who the particular woman is she is first and foremost regarded as a woman. As a consequence, in all too many instances and because of fundamental identity issues there is little perceived fit between her and the executive position.

This is a problem which men in organizations never have to face. A man may perceive that others fail to see him as the right person for a particular job, but he never faces the problem that he is not the person for the job because he is a man. She in contrast has often been "not the person for the job" because she is a woman and little consideration has ever been given to the damage done to her self-confidence when she is forced to confront the negative fit. Who *is* she? For example, if in relationship A there is a negative fit between the woman executive's self-concept and her perception of how others see her, one inevitable result must be concern, worry, anxiety. Her self-confidence falters. Perhaps she isn't who she thinks she is if others don't see her in that light. In relationship B—the relationship between the way in which the woman executive sees herself and the way in which she defines the executive role—a positive fit contributes to her confidence in her own ability to do the job. A negative fit does damage not only to her self-confidence but to the self-ideal she has sought to develop. Perhaps that job is a man's job. Perhaps she was wrong to consider it. Perhaps she should change her objectives and hopes and aspirations to something more fitting. Her image of herself as a potentially successful executive is severely altered if not abandoned.

A basic problem for women in organizations, this issue would probably be clearer in illustration. Let us assume that Jane Smith has a comparatively clear concept of herself and her abilities. She perceives what in reality others think of her and she finds a fit. A management position opens up which in her judgment could provide her with a real opportunity. She can do the job and she wants to do the job. It fits with the person she knows she is. She discusses the requirements of the job with a number of executives in the organization and discovers that they see her, and the job, in more or less the same way as she does. She now feels that she is definitely capable of doing the job. It will be satisfying and rewarding and will provide her with an opportunity for career growth and development. She decides to apply. She is told that she will not even be considered. How does she deal with this? There would seem to be little she could do to effect any change at all.

Yet there is a small number of highly successful women executives in this country, among them the group of twenty-five. How were they able to deal with this problem and the issues that underlie it? What did they do to effect change? That they must have acted in some way is evident, because if one cannot find a positive fit between the way one perceives others as seeing one and the role one is playing, it is very difficult to achieve any tangible success.

These questions were to provide an important key to understanding the achievement of the group of twenty-five and they provide the rationale for basing this study on the perceptions of the woman executive, rather than on some other measure which might possibly have given a less biased report of reality. For a woman in an executive position to succeed she may have to perceive congruence in all of these relationships whether in others' realities that congruence exists or not.

This issue brings the question of behavioral style to the forefront. Again, it is a term that was very simply used. It refers to behavior in a work situation which appeared to contribute to these women's executive success. Studies of male executive behavior have shown that corporate presidents and vice-presidents spend from two thirds to three fourths of their time dealing with interpersonal relations in some form. They must interact with at least five different groups of people: bosses, peers, junior executives, other workers and clients; and this, in addition to all of the "others" in their work and non-work lives. Since the crucial issue for a woman may lie in getting others to accept *any* woman, however superior, in what they consider to be an exclusively male role, behavioral style is a factor even more critically important to women executives than it is to men.

An individual's behavioral style is of course more than behavior. It suggests a general way in which a person tends to behave, given similar stimuli and similar situations. For example, the response patterns of the men and women in management whom we discussed in Part I give rise to very different pictures of the people involved. If we translate the men's responses into behavioral styles we see people who appear to be clearer as to their objectives, who convey a greater understanding of how organizations work both formally and informally, who seem more prepared to pay the costs which winning career rewards requires; who seem, overall, to achieve a better fit between the management environment and themselves. If we think for a moment of the women's responses, a different picture emerges. It is certainly less clear, less certain of the environment.

The patterns of response which individuals develop serve both conscious and unconscious goals and conflict can arise if these two sets of goals are different and one makes no attempt to bring that difference to the surface and deal with it. In such a situation an individual's behavioral style often becomes rigid as a means of coping with the underlying anxiety that conflict gives rise to. He or she responds less to the demands of a given situation and much more to internal pressures to behave in set, fixed ways. This is not to say that individuals do not develop basic, enduring behavioral styles. They do. But behavioral skill lies in becoming particularly adept at adjusting and modifying one's basic style to meet the demands of specific situations.

The issues for analysis in the group of twenty-five were thus commonality of experience; the process of career choice; self-concepts and self-ideals; and the styles of behavior developed by these women in seeking to deal with the additional factor of cultural and social bias against them in the management setting.

As a group, these women were clearly "different" and there is a commonly held belief that such difference is negative. In general the stereotype of the woman executive is unfeminine—she is supposed to be aggressive, masculine, hard, cold and undesirable to men. A proposition developed from such a point of view would state that a successful woman cannot be a successful executive and a successful woman executive cannot be a successful woman. Many men—and women—implicitly believe this. Another commonly held belief is that women are biologically unfit for executive work and here the proposition would doubtless state that a successful woman executive must be biologically lacking in femininity. Just as many men—and women—implicitly believe this. Either way, the difference from the "average" woman is negative.

There is no doubt that the twenty-five *are* different. They differ from any average cross section of American women. But rather than accept stereotypes, assumptions, and the judgments stemming from them about what the difference might be, it is surely more useful to identify what those differences are, how they developed and whether they helped these women lead lives that they could say were both satisfying and rewarding.

The search began with the attempt to find answers to a number of questions.

At every stage in their lives critical relationships must have been established, critical events must have taken place and critical questions must have arisen and been dealt with by these women. What were they and how were they dealt with in childhood and adolescence, in college, during the early career years and in maturity? How did the critical relationships, events, issues and questions arising at each stage affect the stages following? To what extent did the experiences of one life stage influence the over-all developmental pattern of their careers? What, if any, critical issues pervade them all and how do they relate to the development of individual personality and maturity?

The search moved into new territory using as departure points the conclusions of earlier researchers:

Several years ago we decided that a separate theory of career development was needed for men and women . . . We are coming to think that the kind of resolution a woman achieves of her sex role is of major importance in her career.[3]

Most research concerning psychological characteristics and employment, for example, is based on men, and if women are studied at all—which they often aren't—the emphasis is on the extent they differ from men.[4]

As far as this study was concerned, other women were the norm, not men, and a major question had to be why and how these twenty-five particular women were able to achieve highly responsible executive positions at a time when neither legal nor social pressures were there to help them. What was it about them as people—what was it about their experience, behavior and the environments in which they lived and worked—that allowed them to succeed in what, much more then than now, was defined as a "man's world"? What were their personal gains, their inevitable personal losses?

A major assumption was that their accounts of their own experience would be the best source of explanation for the questions raised.

A major objective was to use their private realities to find meaning that would lead to a more general understanding of the broad issue of career development for women.

6

Childhood

In their study of the women enrolled in the M.B.A.
program at Harvard Business School in the year
1963–64, Hennig and Hackman found that there was
a particularly strong and regular pattern to the family
histories of their subjects: twenty out of twenty-five
were either eldest or only children; five were not first-
born but on examination their experiences were essentially similar to those of a first-born child. This was
so for a variety of reasons: death of the eldest brother
or sister, a large age difference between the subject
and an older child, or changes in the family, for instance divorce, which moved the younger child into
the position of an only child. All had had extremely
close relationships with their fathers and had been involved in an unusually wide range of traditionally
masculine activities in the company of their fathers,
beginning when they were very young. They believed
that they had been given unusually strong support by
their families in following their own interests regardless
of the sex-role attributes of those interests. Finally,

they thought that they had developed a very early preference for the company of men rather than of women.[1] These findings were in many ways precursors of what study of the twenty-five would reveal.

All of the twenty-five women in the Hennig study were born in the United States between 1910 and 1915. All were first-born children. Each was destined to be an only child or the eldest in an all-girl family of no more than three children. All were born into upwardly aspiring middle-class families living on or near the eastern seaboard. The fathers of twenty-two of the twenty-five held management positions in business. The other three were college administrators. Twenty-four of the twenty-five mothers were housewives. One mother worked as a teacher. The educational level reached by twenty-three of the mothers was at least equal to that of the fathers and in thirteen cases the mother's education was in fact superior to the father's. The parents' education ranged from high school diplomas to the doctorate, which was held by two fathers. All of the twenty-five and their parents were American-born Caucasians but no distinctive pattern existed in their religious preference of ethnic heritage.

Although they were all first-born this finding might not have held true if a larger population had been available and more women had been studied. For this reason it would probably be more accurate, and certainly more useful, to think of the behavioral dynamics which underlie the early experiences of the first-born child as "special," rather than as exclusively the experience of an eldest child. A child may or may not be first-born—what seems to be critically important is whether he or she receives the special treatment traditionally reserved for the first-born for this sense of specialness contributes heavily to the character of childhood's experience.

All of the twenty-five remembered their childhoods as having been happy. They spoke again and again of the closeness and warmth of their relationships with their parents and from the beginning they felt they assumed a special role in their parents' eyes. They were all only children for at least the first two years of their lives and those who became eldest children were the eldest of no more than three girls.

In describing their early relationships with their parents the twenty-five shared strikingly similar recollections of their fathers.

One of the group said:

"Mother was mother as far as I can recall— hovering over yet encouraging me on. She was always a warm home when I was in trouble, yet she was a strong disciplinarian—she never let me get away with too much. As I think back Father was really something special. As far as I can recall, I was Daddy's special girl. There were always special times set aside for him and me to be alone. When I was very young, he would take me places on Saturday afternoons. He was a very active man and I was always expected to be active with him. In the winter we would go sledding and skating. He taught me to skate when I was four and he used to show me off to all his friends who had sons older than me. 'See,' he would say, 'you may think she is just a girl, but watch her outskate these boys of yours.' I always enjoyed these sessions, and afterward we would go to a soda fountain and have hot cocoa and he would praise me and brag about me to the druggist or anyone else who would listen."

Another woman recalled:

"My dad was a railroad executive, and when I was very young he was supervising some line building in Pennsylvania. Often he got called out on weekends and he would take me along. I am probably the only woman alive who walked railroad tracks under construction at the age of five! Sometimes we would walk several miles, stopping here and there to talk with work crews. Sometimes we would ride on the work trains. They were always warm and smoky, filled with sweating and dirty men. I loved those times, and all the men knew me and talked to me. My dad was very proud of me and often joked with the men about me becoming the first woman train engineer. They would all laugh and then he would get very serious and say that he didn't know what I would do but since I took after him I'd do something famous and unusual."

Still another said:

"I think my dad never stopped hoping for a son but in the meantime I think he singled me out for the role. It was only after I was older that I realized that all girls didn't do the same things with their fathers that I did. Dad was fascinated by two subjects: finance and sports. I was introduced to both before I ever went to school. Dad would read the financial pages to me and go to great pains to explain. I didn't know what he was talking about, but it excited him and I caught that excitement and was always determined to understand it one day. He made me an avid sports lover. My mother really was unathletic so Dad cultivated me as his sports partner. I went to my first boxing match before I went to school.

We fished and later we hunted together. Dad used to take me to a fishing club for weekends and I remember sleeping in a crib. There were all men there but me. I think the men thought that Dad was a bit odd but it never seemed to bother him. He always called me Butch and I never realized the significance of that till much later. We were very close."

Shared in essence by all of the women, these statements point to the existence of a very special relationship between the young girls and their fathers. Fathers and daughters shared interests and activities traditionally regarded as appropriate only for fathers and sons: physical activity, the acquisition of outdoor skills, an aggressive wish to achieve and finally a willingness to compete. Often her father's approval depended on the little girl's ability to succeed or to win. Yet this was done in such a way that the means remained as enjoyable as the end and reward was found in being physically involved and extended. One woman said:

"It's funny how to this day, I really enjoy hard physical activity and physical competition of any kind. I think this goes back to my days of tennis playing with my dad. He taught me when I was very young and he always told me that when I set foot on the court, I should play to win—that was the name of the game, to win. One of the most exciting feelings in the whole world is to work or play so physically hard at winning that you think you are about to collapse and then, at that last second before desperation, you win."

The father-daughter relationship provided an added dimension to these women's childhoods. From it they drew attention, approval, reward and confirmation. It was an added source of early learning, a very early means of expanding their experience, and through it they gained a role model with which they could begin to identify. While they rarely referred to their fathers as having influenced their developmental role as girls, they said that their fathers added to their definition of themselves as people. To their fathers, they were girls. But they were girls who could do much more than girls ordinarily did.

Their memories of their mothers were not as rich in detail, and the mother-daughter relationship was the most elusive to capture and characterize. The following passage is typical:

"The only way that I can really ask myself whether there was anything special about my early relationship with my mother is to think of anything Mother and I did that was very different. I would say we had an average mother-daughter relationship. Mother always cared for me, both physically and emotionally. She always thought it very important that I learn all the feminine ways. I was a very attractive little girl, which always seemed to please Mother. I think that sometimes she got a little upset with Dad for encouraging me to be too independent and competitive—especially when I was very small—but she never really made a fuss about it. I guess she accepted it because it made him happy. Dad and Mother respected each other tremendously. I think they shared so many aspirations for me that they figured that the more each of them could work on me, the better chance I would have to succeed in life."

This passage in fact gives a much clearer picture of the mother-father relationship than it does of the mother-daughter relationship it was supposed to provide. The twenty-five tended to make this shift whenever discussion of their mothers arose. They emphasized repeatedly that both parents held their aspirations for their daughters so much in common that neither parent felt compelled to compete with the other in winning the little girl over to a particular point of view. They said that their parents respected themselves and each other and supported and reinforced the child in developing her own qualities and capacities.

But the problem remained that the women's recollections of the mother-daughter relationship were vague and generalized. They consistently reported that their mothers were "typical," and it became crucial to know what "typical" really meant. To these women it evidently meant that their mothers had done "the right mother-type things." One woman said, "My mother was a warm, fluffy pillow, not terribly exciting, while my father was always dynamic, a really charismatic personality." In general, their mothers were remembered as rather quiet people who exerted their influence from time to time, but who usually gave in to the final wishes of their husbands. They believed that their parents saw each other in much the same way.

For each of the twenty-five their "typical" mother provided a warm, caring and socially sanctioned feminine model, a model they shared with their peers, while their fathers supported them and confirmed them in believing that these were not binding models of behavior but a matter of choice and option—and that the roles themselves could be readily modified. In many ways their fathers opened up a new world for them—a world that replaced and compensated for the old world lost when the early bond to their mothers dissolved, a world that shielded them from ever having to accept that simply because they were girls they necessarily took second place in the order of things.

As little girls they were free to take part in activities usually reserved for little boys. While their mothers confirmed them as little girls, their fathers confirmed their freedom to be more than the traditional little girl was allowed to be and this very early confirmation of their right to do and be more than the traditional role reserved for little girls remained with them throughout their careers.

As they grew older their choice of role slowly came to be seen as an either/or dichotomy between their father's and their mother's roles, a problem that remained unresolved until much later. First apparent when they left the closeness of their families to start out to school, the masculine/feminine role dichotomy became increasingly clear in adolescence, in college and early in their careers. It was a dichotomy forced upon them by the larger society of which they had necessarily to become a part, but their later ability to work through the conflict it presented, to synthesize their own concept of themselves and what they could do with society's traditional view of women, depended heavily on that first crucial confirmation of their right to be more than tradition and society prescribed.

Research indicates what closeness in a family can mean. Douvan and Adelson found that parents in a small family more often shared values which stressed personal responsibility and individual achievement for their children. They found that children in small families of fewer than three siblings:

Were close to both parents.

Identified strongly with parents.

Spent more leisure time with parents.

Used parents as confidants.

Were more likely to absorb the parental point of view.

Were more apt to express trust as a basis of parental relations.

Felt more encouraged to be autonomous.

Were less concerned about peer evaluations.

Were more internalized and more independent.

Were more exploring and risk taking.[2]

One woman captured every one of these issues—and more, for she identified the parent who expressly encouraged autonomy, independence, exploration and the ability to deal with risk.

"From my earliest recollections my parents and I were friends. Of course we like each other, but we loved each other very much. I always wanted to be just like my mother and just like my father, something which I am sure gave those hearing me say it no end of private amusement! Yet in spite of this I think my parents really encouraged me to be myself. They always encouraged me to think through things very carefully and to venture my own opinion, even when I was very very young. I think they really trusted me and I them. It was as if we all dared venture out on our own, because no matter what happened, we would all come together again and we all preferred each other anyway. In some ways they were overprotective; for example, my parents tended to keep me from unpleasantness. Yet in other ways they encouraged me to try things even when I might get hurt. I think, perhaps in my early years they were more protective of my feelings than of my physical safety. I don't mean they would let me kill myself, but the idea of a cut or even a broken bone didn't panic them. I remember wanting to climb a very tall tree when I was about five. My dad said it was too tall for me but I could try if I insisted. My mother said that I would fall. My dad said that if I fell I would learn a good lesson about where my limits were but if I made it I'd learn not to always let others set limitations for me. I climbed that tall tree right straight to the top and I never forgot the lesson."

The meaning of experiences like this can readily be inferred from Douvan and Adelson's list of small-family characteristics. Within very broad limits this woman was in fact learning to be a person as against being taught behavior appropriate only for little girls. Her closeness to her father, his support, the choices he gave her were all helping her grow and develop autonomously while both parents' values were being subtly offered and weighed. She was learning that authority was not a capricious power but was guided by reason and affection. Her parents were friends rather than superiors or autocrats. Most important of all, as a little girl she was being encouraged to take risk and to experience its results. Her father was giving legitimacy to risk-taking, offsetting the possibility of loss with the possibility of gain. Where her mother saw risk in typically negative terms, terms which made the very act itself a negative ("You will fall"), her father was moving her beyond fear as a first emotional reaction, to an early attempt at evaluation of possible outcomes. He was asking her very simply to use her mind.

Her mother's reaction—traditional, typical and understandable—is a clear example of the way in which women transmit a fear of risk to each other. One hears a mother telling a daughter—even as our own have told us and theirs have told them—that risk has as its result only potential for damage, loss, hurt or pain. Given the number of times one sees the transmission of this singularly negative interpretation of risk from a mother to a daughter, it is more than likely that a conscious fear of risk is no longer involved—mothers react in this way toward their daughters because that is the way it has always been. And risk as a consequence is interpreted by women to women as a cultural concept in which reality is rarely tested although all of its dangers in magnified form are assumed to exist. Passed on from woman to woman with no recognition of its implications—and no clear need to do so—nothing could be less helpful in fitting women for management careers.

To see risk as a consequence of judgment based on experience rather than as an issue burdened by the near certainty of personal loss has traditionally been a man's heritage, not a woman's. In the father's response to his small daughter there is the notion that risk is either an opportunity or a cost, a gain or a loss, that it can be injury or it can be growth. For every one of the twenty-five little girls who apparently learned this lesson, there must have been countless others who never did, for it would have been a rare father who thought of teaching his daughter his own response to risk and an equally rare mother who, as these apparently did, would have permitted it.

The sense of trust and security demonstrated by this woman was shared by all of the others. The openness of their relationships with their parents encouraged them at a very early age to deal with adults on a person-to-person basis, and most of them said that as small children they were more comfortable with adults than with their peers. They saw this as an advantage. They felt that the one-sidedness of their early relationships—their strong preference for adults and their lack of interaction with children of their own age —far from representing a loss had given them a head start over other children in the grown-up behavioral skills they acquired. They were much more confident in dealing with authority figures like teachers than were other little girls. And there may have been yet another advantage, for had they had to cope with peer group relationships at this point in their lives the pressure to adapt to the conventional little girl's roles of 1910/1920 might well have upset the clarity of the picture they were forming of their world.

Still these are individual recollections of a long-past reality. Research by a number of child psychologists and child psychiatrists suggests that they must have suffered losses as well as gains in this period of their lives. They were more skilled than other little girls, but were they liked? And if they weren't, what did that mean to them. Relying as they did on the confirmation and approval they won at home, they nonetheless had to cope with a "sudden need" to develop quite different skills in order to deal with their peers after they entered school. Until they were able to master the problems of peer relations they remembered often feeling excluded and uncomfortable. For an extended period later in their lives they were to experience difficult relationships with peers at work and far greater ease in their relationships with their bosses. They finally dealt with this problem by deliberately changing their behavioral styles. They may well have had working for them this early proof that behavioral change was not only possible but rewarding.

Their elementary school years were a time of high

achievement. Typically the twenty-five were at the head of their class and they believed they were social leaders as well. They were members of many organizations and clubs, Brownies, Campfire Girls, 4-H clubs, church groups, school organizations, in which they rose to positions of leadership. Many were elected class president. Team games were important to all of them and they remembered the deep dissatisfaction they felt over the restrictions placed upon them at the elementary level. One woman said:

"By the time I went to elementary school I was a good junior tennis player and was quite proficient at baseball—hardball not sissy softball. I found little girls playing at softball very dull and always tried to wander over where the boys were playing. The boys liked me to play because I was good and I liked being the only girl. The teachers were terribly bothered by this. I guess they thought that I was developing abnormally or something. Finally, one sent a note home asking my folks to make me play with the girls. My dad swore up and down when he read it and called her a frigid bitch. It was years before I knew what that meant, but I knew that he was mad. I don't know what my mother thought. I don't think she got involved. My dad wrote back saying that I could play with the boys and what did she have against boys anyway. I was thrilled and kept playing with the boys off and on until we went to high school. There I met some other girls who were just as good as I was and I gave up masculine sports. I was starting to date anyhow, and I would have stopped for that reason."

From what they were able to remember these women started school with no awareness of the masculine character attributed to sports because they had not been taught at home to distinguish activities along a sexual continuum. They said they learned that sex distinctions had to be made only when they grew old enough to go to school and they learned these through peer group experiences and the attitudes and comments of their teachers. Nonetheless the distinctions they learned to make were inconsistent with their parents', particularly their fathers', points of view, and disagreements between the outside world and the family were always resolved by accepting the parental position. One woman remembered her own conflicting situation in these terms:

"My experience in the early grades of school was a constant frustration. I came into school with the advice of my parents to try everything and do my best at anything that I took part in. To work hard, to do my best and to succeed were the highest values. What confused me in school was that it was acceptable for a girl to do this in some areas but not in all areas. It was okay to be the top in schoolwork, but girls were supposed to compete passively, especially socially. I was being consistently explained away by some adults as a tomboy. I could never understand which activities were boys' and which were girls'. At least I couldn't understand the reasons for the differences. Finally, I developed a skill at remaining within the acceptable girls' activities but steered myself toward those roles which were most active and responsible. I was what was called a girl leader."

By the age of six these women had begun to distinguish sexual identity on the basis of physical appearance and by the age of twelve they were all aware of an enforced distinction on the basis of role. But the concept of innate sexual difference was not very real and as a consequence it was particularly difficult for them as girls in whom a preference for activity had been expressly developed to accept sex-role justifications and explanations which emphasized the feminine role as a passive one. They discussed their recollections of themselves at seven or eight at great length and their reports were notably consistent with each other. One woman stressed the incomprehension which affected them all:

"As I look back, I always liked to do the things that boys did—I liked to do things that girls did too. Actually, I liked to do some of what each did; that is, I wanted to be able to do what I wanted to do. I always knew that I was a girl in that I was pretty, wore dresses, was like my mother and would someday get married and have children. I didn't know what that all meant. I don't think I objected to being a girl or any of the things that girls did; I objected to what people said that girls didn't do. I thought kids ought to be able to do what they wanted to do instead of what they were supposed to do. My parents always supported that idea for me. Of course, at that age I didn't know about that other magic level of sex and boys and girls. That came later, around twelve or thirteen. When I was little I could never understand *why mothers could scrub floors but not play baseball, why they could do all kinds of heavy work at home but not be able to carry the grocery bundles at the store or open their car door when men were around."*

It would be difficult to overestimate the importance of what lies behind this statement: it is a rare little girl who in the course of growing up even notices the inconsistencies inherent in traditional role definitions. It is an even rarer little girl who questions them. The great majority of little girls fail to notice the inconsistencies, for no one around them notices them either. Accepted unthinkingly as "rules," as "the way things have always been," they provide a near schizophrenic background to women's early experience. The fact that the twenty-five noticed, questioned and were unwilling simply to submit to the "rules" was critical to their ability to continue to do so into adulthood—and, in the process, to their ability to define who they were and what they could do in ways that differed significantly from the stereotype.

As ten- and eleven-year-olds they thought of themselves as successful, able and yet somehow frustrated and limited. They thought that they were basically happy, somewhat arrogant toward their peers and held in high esteem by their parents and teachers. They conceived of themselves as little girls but felt that boys had the better of the two worlds because of the greater freedoms society allowed. Largely due to their fathers' influence, their lives at home were free of the role restrictions they were increasingly aware of in life outside the family. They were not at all clear as to how to cope with this basic conflict and they simply believed they would be better off in the world of boys. One woman put this vividly:

"When I was ten, I was a boy in a girl's body—I was convinced of this. I knew I was a girl, I knew what the anatomical differences were and all that, but that wasn't what bothered me; it was the fact that boys had all the freedom and all the fun. The code of living which was being taught and encouraged at home was not fitting the experiences I was having outside. Since my home ties were far stronger than anything outside, I persisted in my devotion to being a boy. Yet, I was also unhappy doing so, because I wanted to be generally liked and respected—another important family code. It took me a long time to work out a way of thinking about myself that encompassed being a girl and being successful and active. For success, as it was defined by my parents, was not just success at the traditional girl's things but also success in ways which it seemed only boys were allowed to achieve. When I first started school there wasn't much made of this in terms of boys and girls, but by the fifth and sixth grades, we began to be carefully differentiated. Boys were mathematical and scientific, while girls were artistic and musical. Girls did well in English, but boys did well in civics. There were many more subtle distinctions than subject matter or gym. Girls' social activities were basically social, while boys would have projects and achievements. They could be task-oriented. To me, girls' groups were a waste of time. Basically, they sat around and talked and I wanted to be more active and do things once in a while. Actually so did a lot of the girls, because I always ended up as the leader of girls' organizations because I got them to do something once in a while."

Fundamental requirements for succeeding at *anything* include the drive to achieve, an orientation to task, the desire to be respected for one's abilities, the enjoyment of competition, a capacity to take risk. These are qualities as much sought after in business executives as in administrators of non-profit organizations. They are qualities which are widely regarded as masculine and thus as appropriate only for men. In this case, they are qualities which twenty-five little girls demonstrably possessed and which they regarded as high in value to them, rewarding in themselves and capable of earning them the confirmation and esteem of their parents and in particular, the esteem of their fathers.

Yet these little girls developed so-called masculine qualities and objectives without abandoning their naïve definitions of themselves as female. Rather they found their girlhood confining, they fought the role for greater freedom, their fathers actively supported them and their mothers' tacit permission shielded them from the sense of conflict which her opposition would have ensured. Their reaction to boys was not one of envying male sexuality but rather one of jealousy at the far fewer constraints placed on the behavior of boys. These women in fact were asking to be more than the prescribed roles of "girl" would allow them. Given their fathers' values they found the traditional girls' role to be intolerably restrictive and their parents' support gave them the security they needed to challenge accepted role restrictions. While they did so only in small ways, their experience was nonetheless one of challenge, with conflict resulting, followed by attempts at resolving it—with all of these issues centering on their ability to be girls and yet more than girls were supposed to be.

Their experience at such an early age helps explain

why they were later able to challenge the male world of management in ways that enabled them to enter that world themselves. To succeed, they needed support and confirmation even as their parents had supported them and confirmed them in the past. They found that support—and it was vitally important to their careers. But most important of all, their past made them confident enough that they would find it to risk making the search.

One begins to see in the experience of these women that many of the characteristics traditionally considered to be masculine, sometimes regarded as innate masculine traits, might better be understood if they were seen as based on knowledge, skill and competence which boys develop by virtue of the kinds of activities and relationships in which they engage, the ways of thinking to which they are exposed and the rewards they win for mastery of any of these things. Looking at the early lives of the twenty-five one begins to see that as little girls, they were able to share in a learning experience, and to be rewarded for their success at mastering it, that is not the usual learning experience even of today's little girls and which in the decade after 1910 was even further from the norm. One might well conclude that much of what is referred to as "masculine thinking" may be a body of learning and knowledge acquired by one half of our children in an entirely unstructured class room whose subject matter differs radically from that to which the other half is exposed.

7

Adolescence

Adolescence for the twenty-five as it is for us all was dominated by a major theme: the emergence of sexual identity and the attempt to cope with the problems to which it gives rise. The stability of their home lives and the encouragement and support of their parents, particularly of their fathers, had helped them earlier to live with the conflicts arising over their concept of themselves, of the people they were trying to be, and what society was already saying they should be. With the coming of adolescence new and deeper conflicts occurred.

The data collected on this period in the women's lives revealed that between the ages of twelve to thirteen they were growing acutely aware of their gender and of the limitations it imposed. Where earlier they relied on their parents' approval and were willing and able to ignore the conflicts which developed between their sense of themselves and societal expectations, as adolescents they found it increasingly difficult to continue to do so. In adolescence the confirmation and support which their families had given them became less and less useful. Their established sense of security was threatened and their ideas of who they were became more and more dependent on the attitudes and opinions of others outside the family. They spent less time at home and more in the world of their peers, and it was far less helpful now than earlier to have Father or Mother say that something was "all right" when friends and teachers said it wasn't. More specifically there were some things that Mother was beginning to say were *not* "all right."

All of the twenty-five emerged out of family backgrounds in which the assumption of feminine inferiority did not apply to them as individuals. They were a group of human beings with a very early experience of freedom, of the right to self-expression and to the development of an identity beyond accepted role restrictions. As they grew, their roles outside the home became more and more circumscribed. Relationships outside the family grew increasingly important and in adolescence, confronted by their own developing sexual identity, it became more difficult for them to oppose the pressures of their own small worlds. More obviously than ever they were girls and now more strongly than ever were expected to act accordingly.

Many of the women talked at length about this issue and the following passage is typical:

"Physiological sex became acutely obvious to me when I began to realize some relationship between boys and freedom. At the same time my mother was trying to convince me of the need for girls to be protected from any possibility of becoming pregnant. I suddenly realized why society let boys be free while I was expected to become confined and constrained. Believe me, at the time

I hated like hell not just having a male body; that's what it meant to me—the difference in body. To me, boys and girls were the same people except for that and the way they and society chose for them to act. The only clear distinction I could accept was the physical one, and that in itself never made any difference to me until I realized the vulnerability against which the female had to protect. I wonder how the pill will change all of this eventually?

"After that, and before I had even known the experience, I really resented the fact that I was supposed to deny myself the pleasure of being sexually free. Oh, my mother tried to convince me that it wasn't anything for women anyway, but I was already reading too many books to believe that!

"I think that first I felt that society had done me in by creating me 'female.' Then it was my parents, then women, and finally my mother whom I blamed. I can remember reasoning that I had an equal chance of being either sex, and it had to be my mother's fault that I was a girl. How was that for reasoning? A lot of hostility developed between Mother and me—my resenting her for making me a girl and she trying even harder to make me into one. I had a lot of trouble understanding what I saw as a major shift in her attitude toward me. For the first ten years she encouraged me to be free, and now when I was old enough to appreciate it and use it, she was cracking down."

At first sight this statement may appear to be a classic description of the indiscriminately applied theory of penis envy: it may seem to set the background for the onset of the so-called "last battle for masculinity" and to describe the dynamics—increased hostility toward the mother who has injured the girl, causing her to be less than a boy.

Yet this woman is talking about vulnerability and constraint, both of which describe societal conditions not of her making. She is not talking about a drive to require masculinity for itself alone. She is talking about restrictions being placed upon the person she knows she is, upon her identity, upon her concept of herself as a free and autonomous person.

Freudian interpretations of femininity would entirely evade this issue by asserting that this woman's conscious objections to her own vulnerability and to the constraints to which it gave rise were the outcome of an unconscious drive to be sexually a man. The sudden reversal of the independent trend of her development so far and the bewilderment and conflict arising as a result would then be explained away on the grounds that from the very first she wished sexually to be a boy, possessor of a penis, recipient of the greater sexual satisfaction which at a much earlier developmental stage she was supposed to be capable of imagining boys enjoyed. She would now be seen as engaging in that fateful, final battle for masculinity in which every other aspect of her identity was overwhelmed, and the factors which formed that identity, preeminently the special quality of the parent-child relationship, would never be seen at all. Such an analysis would ignore a crucially important issue: that these women again and again attested to the fact that they enjoyed being girls, little girls who were "special" and whose fathers made them "special" by taking them into the world of men. That they wanted to continue to be girls who shared and indeed expanded upon the roles they could play in a man's world is, from their later history, an explanation grounded in both fact and common sense.

Had this woman abandoned her own needs and given in to those of her mother she would have had to modify her earlier orientation to activity, competition and achievement—an orientation based on values that are critical to the performance of many executive roles. The group of twenty-five abandoned neither their values nor their earlier orientation and their behavior as a result differed sharply from what has traditionally been considered "normal" in adolescent girls.

Feminine normalcy has been defined in terms of its distance from the masculine norm—the further the better—and some of the accepted polarities are: active vs. passive; aggressive vs. submissive; creative vs. sustaining; risk-taking vs. security-seeking; strong vs. gentle; taking vs. receiving. From the onset of puberty girls and boys are expected to begin the search for partners and to learn how to behave in those partnerships in the adult world. These distinctions offer a clear, socially sanctioned behavioral prescription which for women has meant accepting a role that was passive, submissive, sustaining, security-minded, gentle and receptive—characteristics that in the 1920s would have been even more widely viewed as essential to the achievement of adult femininity.

Since society and psychology alike have traditionally agreed on these role components, the group of twenty-five presents an enlightening deviation from the norm. What gave them the sense of freedom and security they needed to continue in activities and roles not usually considered feminine? How did they succeed in seeing themselves as people for whom the traditional women's roles represented only a part of life? What were the gains and losses they met with?

In following these women through adolescence one finds evidence of a determined struggle not to be submerged by the restricted, confining woman's role and on this basis their hostility and resentment toward their mothers emerged. They came to see their mothers as having given up the struggle and as attempting now to force them to do the same. In sharp contrast to these developments all of them reported that their relationship with their fathers remained much as it had always been. One woman said:

"This was a time for reducing dependency on my mother, for rejecting some of her—and other women's—traditional ideas about women's roles. My relationship with Dad changed very little. Perhaps it broadened and deepened, if anything. I was always a center of Dad's attention. Dad valued individual achievement and accomplishment above all else in life. Dad never looked at Mother and me as similar. He expected and rewarded one kind of behavior in my mother and another in me.

"Oh, sure, he treated me with some new style, he complimented me more on my appearance. But basically we continued to be very good friends. We still played tennis, sailed together in the summer and discussed his business interests with real vigor. When I was thirteen, I began to work for Dad in his office. I think that this was also about the time that I decided I didn't like women on general principles! That is, I didn't like to be with women. They made me feel very uncomfortable, but I also disapproved of them. I thought they were stupid and I always thought they felt the same about me! I had certain girl friends with whom I shared common interests, but that was all."

Another woman said:

"When I was about twelve, I decided that my mother wasn't really all I had her stacked up to be. I remember it was a terrible crisis in my life. I think it all began after she began to suggest that I give up my tomboy status. She said I should settle down and learn to become a young lady— that word 'learn' struck me! I thought it was very nice to be a young lady but not the way my mother meant it. She meant being a 'young lady.' I looked upon myself as a person. I thought that it was unfortunate that I wasn't a boy, only because it would have made things easier for everyone. I remember blaming her for that, too. I began to have some problems with my friends at that time too. I had a few close girl friends, but I hated groups of girls. I always preferred one-to-one relationships. I also began to get into co-ed social activities and that ended all-girl organizations for me! I preferred being vice-president of a mixed group to president of a girl's anything. My dad was so steadfast during this crisis, he stayed good old Dad, and our relationship was my harbor in the storm."

Typically, children are encouraged to identify with and imitate adults of the same sex and boys soon learn that certain qualities, skills and goals define masculinity, that masculinity is itself rooted in the acquisition of competence and in achievement one can call one's own. Girls tend to learn that the traditional woman's role defines competence in a quite different way: increasingly it becomes competence at marrying a man who *has* competence, who *is* an achiever—and winning him away from the competition of other girls.

For girls, especially for the achievement-oriented among us, adolescence often brings with it a traumatic switch in the definition of competence. Success becomes identified with popularity, with being the most sought-after girl in the group. For boys competence remains what it has always been: objective achievement, success at what you set out to do, emergence as a leader. Certainly it helps to be handsome and popular but if you aren't, competence can help sustain the comforting belief that you will win in the long-term, out there in the world of achievement. For adolescent girls, this tends to be cold comfort indeed. After all, how many women have ever won out there —in that world?

Their untraditional fathers, rather than their increasingly traditional mothers, became critical to the process of identity formation in the adolescent group of twenty-five. By seeing them as women, but as women who were capable of being more than a role, their fathers counteracted the traditional notion of femininity which conflicts directly with achievement, and immeasurably sustained the values with which they had invested objective competence and achievement.

There was a uniqueness to the adolescent father-daughter relationship for all of these women. They did not see themselves as having to compete with their mothers for their fathers' affection nor did they see their mothers as threatening this relationship in any other way. Earlier they had remembered their mothers as comfortable necessities, "warm, fluffy pillows," who were not terribly exciting or magnetic. Now they saw them, sometimes as understandably, but more often as irritatingly old-fashioned.

That they could take their mothers so much for granted was to an incalculable degree due to the absence of sons. These women's adolescent protests against the restrictions their mothers sought to place on them were free of the bitterness that direct comparison with a brother's independence would have evoked and the parent-child relationship was never strained by the jealousy of "They prefer him to me because they let him do things and go places they won't let me."

The absence of sons in the family from the first allowed these women to be "special." The dissolution of the first relationship to their mothers, painful as it would have been, was balanced by their fathers' active interest, attention and love and in coping with their own feelings of loss they never had to contend with cues of any kind from their parents that boys were either preferred, or better, or both. In other words, they could not tie disappointment and rejection to the fact that they were girls, to a fundamental part of their identity, as so many other girls inevitably must. Because of this a critical part of their self-esteem was preserved.

In adolescence they saw their mothers as turning against them, not just because they were girls, but because their mothers would not stand up to social pressures. There is an important difference here. Because of it these women could be certain that there was no defect inherent in themselves because they *were* girls and they could believe that social prescriptions could be challenged if they were prepared to pay the cost.

All of the women said that in adolescence the father-daughter relationship maintained its strong orientation to achievement. Admiration and affection flowed from father to daughter on the basis of objective accomplishment and success. The fathers placed the highest emphasis on their daughters' developing skills and abilities rather than on a socially defined sex role or behavioral style, and when the daughters felt particularly threatened this relationship provided them with great emotional security. In general it was a relationship which heightened their sense of self-esteem and diverted and shielded them from the tensions arising as a result of demands placed upon them to conform.

Yet it would be misleading to view the fathers of these women as treating their daughters exactly as they would have treated sons. There is no evidence to suggest that the fathers in any way rejected their daughters' femininity. They acted toward their daughters as they might have acted toward a son but with a regard for the real sexual identity of the child. In turn, the child did not view her father as needing any special winning over during adolescence since he had been won over years before.

The most important source of support and confirmation of these women's developing self-concepts and their most important source of reward in adolescence lay in this relationship. When everything else around them and about them was changing, their fathers' interest and love remained constant. It was a time when they remembered feeling closer to their fathers than ever before. Where in childhood both parents had given security and reinforcement to their daughter this now became the father's primary role, with the mother seen as a potential source of conflict on the eternal issue of who the girl felt she was and wanted to be, and who society—and her mother—thought she should be. They did not reject the reality of femininity nor did they with any finality reject the person who was

their mother. Rather they rejected the role definition
of femininity which she attempted to impose.

In research on 1,925 adolescent girls Douvan and
Adelson found three distinct patterns of beliefs and
goals which they described as the feminine pattern,
the masculine pattern and the ambivalent pattern.
They described the ambivalent pattern as follows:

> The ambivalent feminine girls combine explicit in-
> tegration of feminine goals with a desire for cer-
> tain aspects of the roles traditionally assigned to
> men. While having drives to marriage and moth-
> erhood, they have a lively interest in personal
> achievement both now and in the future. They
> are highly focused on individual development.
> They give high priority to concerns and fantasies
> about success. They show a great interest in non-
> social skills and jobs. They choose male role mod-
> els more often than female and whoever their
> role model, it is chosen for admirable traits and
> skills—character, talent, work skills and personal
> attractiveness. They choose these objectively,
> while the feminine girls use emotional ties to se-
> lect a model. These girls (the Ambivalents) show
> a remarkable ability to select higher risks in
> choice situations. They have a great readiness to
> rely upon their own resources. Their parents
> treated them as we would expect boys to be
> treated normally. They report that one or more
> parents care most about their skills and independ-
> ence. Good sense and good judgment are highly
> rated family values. The unambivalent girl seeks
> to reach her goal only through marriage while the
> ambivalent girl sees at least two available means
> —individual achievement and marriage.[1]

It is perhaps instructive that just ten years ago the word "ambivalent" was used to categorize girls who essentially sought to bring sexual and intellectual demands together, who sought to become whole human beings. This apart, whatever else the twenty-five may have been at this point in their lives, there is little evidence of ambivalence. Somehow they were going to find ways of dealing with the conflicts they felt. And they knew they could rely on their fathers to help them.

In high school they all did well academically. Co-educational activities offered them a new challenge and they moved into positions of leadership in co-ed organizations, in most cases as second-in-command. Possibly as a consequence they claimed that they dated as frequently as other girls. Eventually they looked forward to marriage and motherhood. A typical statement read:

"It never occurred to me that I would not marry and have children. I just wanted to do more than that. I wanted to be more of a person than my mother was. I knew I was a woman and I enjoyed being admired by boys. But this was in addition to being admired by adults for my accomplishments and skills. My mother and I came to terms after I began to date and show some interest in some of the female things. She even began to enjoy and encourage my successes in school and began to discuss college and career with me. My dad, of course, had no thought other than college as a minimum for me. I was still a rebel in my peer group but my friends seemed to accept me as I was. Anyway we were busy with living and we seldom had time to worry about the future. I did worry some in private and I thought it important that I go to a co-educational college. I thought the usual career choice of teaching or nursing was very limited and thought I might pursue secretarial work in order to work in the same kind of environment I was familiar with through my dad."

This response, apparently casual in its feminine orientation, in fact indicates full acceptance of femininity with the addition of something else, the wish to achieve and to be rewarded for it. Confronted by adolescent pressures to conform to more passive roles, they sought to modify them in favor of their own developing self-concepts. There was a sense of emerging autonomy and self-control in their late adolescent behavior. For the first time they talked openly of their concern for the "fit" between their own needs and goals and the situations in which they would intentionally place themselves. They began to talk of college, and of their plans for a career. Going to work in adulthood did not present itself as an alternative life-style, but as the only and obvious one. One woman said:.

"There was only one thing for certain—I never even considered the idea of getting married and staying home as my mother did. This was a way of life that I must have rejected very early in my life, because I always remember knowing that I did not want a way of life like my mother's but rather like my father's. Work, to me, was an exciting and satisfying activity which I looked forward to excitedly and never considered living without."

The fathers' role in raising their daughters was to this point clear and consistent and culminated with their becoming the primary role model. The mothers, who had begun by encouraging autonomy and achievement and had then changed during their daughters' early adolescence to become active supporters of the traditional and constraining feminine role, changed yet again. All of the twenty-five recalled their mothers' manifest relief when they became interested in boys and began to be concerned with how they looked. They grew closer to their mothers and their mothers in turn began once again to support and confirm the value they placed on achievement.

The mothers in fact had accomplished what they viewed as a major responsibility, the evocation of their daughters' overt recognition of being female, and this done they were then able to return to reinforcing the entire child. This was a crucial contribution to these women's future development, for had their mothers continued to oppose their other interests and had they continued to see the feminine role as totally in conflict with their other aspirations, the twenty-five might well have faced intolerable difficulty in maintaining their still tenuous integration of who they were and what they wanted to be. Had their mothers continued to oppose them and more, had they tried to invoke the aid of the fathers in their opposition, the daughters might well have either submitted or rebelled, and a very different motivational set would have evolved.

Adolescence for these women was in essence a time when, not without real difficulty, they clarified and strengthened their concepts of themselves. They set themseves an ideal in independence and achievement. They accepted femininity and its traditional objectives of marriage and motherhood on their own terms. They determined they would go to college, begin a career and marry later. Their families continued to give them the security they needed but there was evidence of their own growing strength: they rejected their mothers' traditional views and they held firm to their own objectives, relying on their fathers' support and their own inner convictions.

It is as if they were setting the stage for the future. Their choice of their father as a role model, their dislike of "traditional" women, their preference for co-educational activities were predictors of what they would now do: attend a co-ed university; major predominantly in a professionally oriented area rather than in the liberal arts; establish much closer relationships with their male peers than with other women (men would confirm them, women would consider them odd); choose a career related to their fathers, and work almost exclusively in the company of men. All of these choices would be made during college and in the first years of their careers.

8

The College Years

The twenty-five reached college age during the years of the Great Depression. College enrollments were shrinking. Fewer and fewer parents could afford to educate even their sons. Yet for these women there seemed to have been no question that they would do other than go to college. In thinking back to their high school years, none of them could identify when it was that they decided they would go on to college. Most of them said that the decision had never really been made, that since the age of nine or ten going to college had seemed an inevitable part of the life they wanted.

They went in a time of economic crisis when few women received a college education and they took with them an unusually clear view of what they wanted: they wanted preparation for a career choice which in broad terms had already been made. They were going to work. They were going to have careers like their fathers. But despite their individual clarity about what they wanted to do it was to be a more difficult time than any they had yet lived through. They were now almost entirely on their own.

Their environment expanded considerably and they abandoned many of their adolescent fantasies about themselves and their potential. The real-life options open to them were wider and the kinds of people with whom they had to deal were on a broader spectrum. They were farther away from their families than they had ever been before and one of the most pressing tasks before them was to find new sources of personal support and security.

They knew that once again they would confront an environment in which their goals and their plans would be seen as quite different from those of the majority of women they would meet. They were aware that once again conflict would arise over what was expected of them as college women and what they expected for themselves.

The kind of college they chose was consistent with their commitment to a career. In a day when most girls of their socio-economic background preferred to attend private women's colleges, all but one of them selected a co-educational university. They said that they wanted an environment in which they could interact with men and they wanted to be able to study in subject areas which only the presence of men would make available. The majors they chose were as follows:

Major	No. of Women Choosing It	Per Cent
Business	7	28
Economics	5	20
Math	2	8
History	3	12
Secretarial Studies	2	8

Liberal Arts—General	4	16
Other	2	8
	25	100

One woman described her choice of major in the following terms:

"When I got to college, I had to finally commit myself to some area of intensive study. I looked at what was available and discussed it with Dad and Mother and some of my high school teachers and I decided to study business and finance. I knew that if I wanted a business career, I'd probably have to take a secretarial job. Then that was as good as women could start with anyway. Even nurses and teachers and home economics graduates were having trouble getting jobs. I felt that I knew and loved business—at least what I saw as the climate and challenge of it—and my dad had taught me a lot about the practical side already. I was delighted to discover that I was the only woman majoring in business with about three hundred men. I always found the men to be terribly nice and very protective. Oh, there were some SOB types, but I ignored them. There were plenty of guys for me to hang in with who were willing to accept that I was serious. Anyway, I was soon at the top of my classes and my study help was very popular. I think even the SOB types had to respect me and that was all I asked."

All of the twenty-five had already rejected the "traditional feminine woman" as someone to identify with, but their avoidance of this kind of woman was simultaneously a means of defending themselves against being misunderstood or mocked. In the world of fraternity pins they would have had to explain and attempt to justify why they were doing what they were doing, to take yet another look at who they were. In many ways the "traditional woman" threatened the new and different women they sensed themselves to be—and so many women *were* traditional. Suppose both they and their fathers were wrong? Was a career really a man's prerogative? Why had so few women achieved in the world of work? These were the "traditional" questions. They didn't want to think about them, much less try to answer them. They didn't want doubts, they wanted confirmation.

At least some men reinforced them. Some men confirmed that they were both attractive and intelligent even as earlier their fathers had done. Most men were altogether less difficult, less threatening and more stimulating than women. The SOBs could be dealt with because at an intellectual level even their respect could be earned. This was not a level at which they felt they could satisfactorily deal with female SOBs.

Embedded in the relationships they established was an issue of critical importance to their future management success: they already recognized, probably without even questioning why, that it was possible to develop working relationships with men on a basis of competence and intellectual ability, that they did not need to base relationships on personal ties or even necessarily on liking. Where two men might hold positions on a football team, work together successfully during the game and dislike each other throughout, in quite different circumstances they used the same approach.

They said that they discussed what they wanted to do with their parents and that they were influenced by their parents' views, but that the process had not been one of simple compliance with their parents' wishes.

Rather it was one in which their parents reinforced their own inclinations. They said that although they had consciously chosen their fathers as role models this was essentially a private matter which did not arise in their discussions with their parents. Several of them said that for them their father's job was a specific model distinct from the kind of organization in which he worked. The woman whose father was an educational administrator, for example, said that she was attracted to administrative work but not necessarily in an educational setting. Those who chose liberal arts majors said that they did so because their fathers had always regarded a classical education as a necessary foundation for professional training which could and should come at the graduate level. These women nonetheless added economics to their liberal arts work load and, in common with the others, used their fathers as models. The two women who chose secretarial studies believed that their skills would provide them with an established point of entry into the business world and once there, they would learn. Whatever their major, they all saw a relationship between the preparation they believed it would provide and the career they sought.

They all worked hard. Semester after semester they won places on the dean's list and several of them graduated with highest honors and election to Phi Beta Kappa. Through it all they claimed to have led active social lives.

The pattern they established for themselves was one of goal-setting, planning, the establishment of priorities and sub-goals, and commitment to a course of action with distracting diversions identified and avoided. They attempted, as one woman said, to avoid "the temptations of new situations and experiences." What, they effectively asked themselves, was the straightest possible line between where they were and where they wanted to be? In a real sense the pattern they established was a management pattern. An ambitious young man tends to follow it without question. Ambitious young women tend to be born at twenty and the process begins ten years late.

All of the twenty-five rejected sorority living and chose to live in women's halls of residence. They said that they avoided sorority life because it was "traditionally female" and entirely unsupportive of the kind of woman they wanted to be. One woman said:

"I knew that if I accepted an invitation to a sorority, I would end up as the antagonist of the whole group. I didn't believe in the same things they did and I wasn't seeking the best husband as my major goal in college. We simply had nothing in common, those sorority sisters and me! And I knew myself well enough to know that I would be miserable and I'd make them miserable, because I'd be telling them how stupid I thought they were, and they had just as much right to seek their goals in peace as I did. I chose to live in the women's residence. Girls there tended to be more task- and career-oriented like myself and the social life was just as good as that in the sororities. Besides, I just didn't care that much for women; I never did and that's why I chose the co-ed school and a major like business. I was president of my women's residence hall for my last three years, and I did enjoy that job. I was working with girls more like myself. We accomplished a lot in those three years."

Their rejection of women's traditional social goals was by then firmly established. And yet these women were not rejecting *women,* rather they were rejecting women who behaved in traditionally feminine ways and who expected that other women should behave similarly. It was a rejection of a role and a behavioral style rather than of individuals, and emotionally it was grounded in their earlier rejection of their mothers' roles as "traditional women." As a result they were most forceful of all in rejecting feminine interests and pursuits which had as their objective the attraction and acquisition of a husband. They rejected the behavior required—they saw passivity and submission toward men as unnecessary, and worse, as damaging a woman's ability to compete with men in a work setting, a setting entirely different and separate from that of a home and family.

Although the twenty-five identified "traditional women" as their major antagonists from a very early stage in their lives, they rarely mentioned the personal reactions to them of boys, or of men other than their fathers. When finally they began to talk about men in their college years they talked about the "men who were for me and those who were not." They tended to place men in "either-or" categories, the "nice types" and the "SOBs." Just as there were "traditional women" and "career-centered women," the latter like themselves and the former like their mothers, men fell into two categories: those who were supportive like their fathers and those who were not.

Yet, interestingly enough, they were increasingly confident that they could deal with male "SOBs" by leading from their own task-related strengths and allowing friendship to develop as it would. Without really recognizing it, they were rejecting the more internal process in which women, consciously and unconsciously, establish personal liking as a prerequisite for a task-related relationship. In relying on their ability to accomplish tasks as a source of self-confidence, they were developing a style for the future which would allow those whom they did not like, or those who did not like them, to be both tolerated and discounted. They were, in short, developing valuable distance between their ability to appreciate objective skills and subjective evaluations of the people who possessed them.

All of the twenty-five said that they dated regularly during college, and the SOBs notwithstanding, they believed that their relationships with their male peers were generally good. In retrospect they thought that many men did not take their career aspirations seriously enough to be negative about them. At the time, spared such reactions, they simply assumed that they *were* taken seriously. It is entirely possible that they transferred to men in general their perceptions of their fathers' attitudes and opinions. As a consequence they *expected* positive reactions and acted as if they did until they were proven wrong. Much later, their implicit assumption of acceptance rather than of rejection allowed them to deal with men at every hierarchical level in a way which compelled those who felt negatively about them to act first—to raise the issue in a vacuum as a consequence of the individual man's personal difficulties rather than as a consequence of the individual woman's signal that she *expected* negative reactions. In other words they perceived a fit between themselves and the job to be done even when in others' minds it might not be there. In doing so they helped themselves immeasurably and avoided the painful trap which so many individual women fall into —expecting negative reactions she projects her own doubts clearly enough for them to mesh with the doubts already existing in others' minds and so establishes a negative reciprocal which is extraordinarily difficult to break.

Over and above this, yet another dynamic seems to have been at work. By the time they were halfway through college these women's objectives were so obviously different from those of the majority of other women that other women were a potential source of hostility and conflict. Other college women could see that these women had repudiated *their* goals, they were not in search of husbands and anticipating settling down as housewives. The college men, on the other hand, not necessarily believing the twenty-five's seriousness about their career objectives, presented them with much less potential for open conflict.

In the Hennig and Hackman study of *Men and Women at Harvard Business School,* the women participants reported that they first experienced negative reactions from men when they entered the Business School.[1] They said that they sensed some negative attitudes toward them from single men they dated outside the school, but that the strongest negative feedback came from unmarried male students within the school itself. Male students who were married were more supportive.

A woman's presence at a major business school in 1964 represented a much deeper commitment to a future career in business than did attendance at an undergraduate school in the early 1930s. The problem for the single men in the Hennig and Hackman study lay in their realization of that commitment and the uncomfortable contrast it made with the stereotypes they held of women and of themselves. When the group of twenty-five took their next step along the path of career commitment and entered their first jobs they found that male attitudes toward them divided on the same basis—married men tended to see them as persons, single men to see them as out of place! They were clearly there by their own choice and they did not and should not belong.

Three researchers in the field of career development, Super[2] and Tiedeman and O'Hara,[2] have all held that the process of career choice is crucial to future career success or failure, but they took special note of how little research has been directed at discovering what actually takes place at this point in an individual's life. Within this limitation they generally accepted that career choice results from the interaction of a number of important variables: an individual's psychological predispositions, intelligence, skills and talents; socio-economic background and needs; and a progressive testing of the environment. They also suggested that for many people large elements of chance and of unconscious motivation are involved: individuals cannot choose from what they do not know exists or have no way of knowing they would like.

No one has yet been able to determine how these variables measurably combine to result in career choices or even whether they must all be present in every individual case. As a consequence, while the college years are acknowledged to be a critical period, unfortunately it is the period about which least is known. Where women are concerned still less is known, and very little of what *is* known even applies. The extra variable of being a woman and its reflection in whether one is even encouraged to prepare for the job has hardly been considered.

In fact, the important variables identified by career development theorists as part of the process of career choice *for men* have the flavor of a bad, sad joke when considered in relation to women. At a minimum the theorists assume that the individual brings with him knowledge and skill as well as talent and intelligence; that socio-economic pressures have combined to develop aspirations and expectations, a positive disposition toward acquiring an objectively measurable, demonstrable competence, a recognition of the importance of the environment and some definition of what he wants to do and where he wants to go. Given the differences we discussed in Part I of this book, what the theorists have to say is irrelevant to the great majority of women, for it reflects only the male experience.

In general women come to the job setting with no prior knowledge of behavioral norms and expectations, with no concrete recognition of what a career means or the part a job must necessarily play in it, with no clear career aspirations or objectives. Nor do all that many women bring with them a positive disposition toward objectively measurable, demonstrable competence because of their ambivalent experience with this issue as they grew up—after all, did you want to be popular or did you want to be at the head of the class? Narrow horizons inevitably set limits on perception and women's much narrower horizons in terms of what they can do or will do effectively discounts the importance of environments they don't know, and highlight out of all proportion those few they know and are sure of. Faced with difficulty in defining who they are in the management world of men, they are faced with even greater difficulty in defining what they wish to become. Where the theorists suggest that chance exposure can help form and determine career choice one must ask oneself how useful even this is, given the limited kinds of experience and exposure hitherto—and even now—available to adolescent women as far as career possibilities and opportunities are concerned. Ninety per cent of women at work are still clustered in five occupational categories.

From childhood on the twenty-five women in this study were taught, encouraged and supported by fathers, who expected them to aspire to and prepare for a career; who passed on to them their own view of a career as an integral part of a person's life; who dealt with them on the basis of an unquestioned assumption: that they would work, just as a man would do, for the greater part of their adult lives.

Barnett, in her study of Radcliffe College seniors, approached the issue of women's career choices by attempting to identify attitudinal patterns.[4] In a pilot study of her subject group, she tentatively identified three major patterns surrounding the issue of choice, and study of these patterns became the later focus of her research. She described the three attitudinal sets as Internalizers, Identifiers and Compliers.

The Internalizer was a girl whose career goals and personal goals were well enough integrated to allow her to think through a logical career plan for the next five years. Her self-concept and her vocational aspirations were complementary, congruent and directed toward personal and vocational integration. She was found to have strong feminine needs as well as a clear need for vocational activity; however, these needs were independent of each other rather than overlapping and conflicting. She had thought through the implications of both sets of needs with considerable care and she believed herself to be the kind of person who could deal with the implications of both because they represented complementary parts of her personality and self-concept.

The Identifier (about half of the entire group) had more confused future goals. She saw her feminine needs and her career needs as being in conflict with each other and she had an either-or approach to her future. She made her immediate career choice in relation to the person or persons with whom she identified most strongly. She wanted to be in a certain profession because she strongly liked or respected some person who was already in that profession, or she liked the image she had of people in a given career. She thought that she might have a career for a while, then be a wife for a while, then a mother for a while, and then perhaps be a career woman again. But she could see no way of integrating or managing any of these conflicting issues at the same time.

The Complier was a person who was really unable to make any clear personal plans but would do whatever she had to do at the last possible moment. Like the Identifier, her feminine needs and her career needs were seen by her as in conflict, but unlike either of the others, she understood very little about herself in these areas. She was apt to be influenced in deciding her immediate future by whoever exerted the greatest influence or pressure upon her at the time of choice.

The pervasive femininity/achievement conflict as distinct from research on career development has a growing literature of its own. Horner's well-known study highlights the woman undergraduate's painful dilemma over the conflict she perceives to exist between the two issues.[5] Rosenbloom, in a study of women who were both married and employed in middle management jobs, found that for these women coping with the conflicts which arose between their married role and their job role was the major energy absorber of their lives.[6] The majority of these women said that they had had to decide which role should become dominant and then they had had to learn to live with it. The majority predicted that eventually they would have to give up one or the other—if they remained at work they would try to move as far ahead as they could, and if they did so they could see no way in which they would have time or energy left for maintaining a marriage.

Among the four other groups of women who formed a subsidiary focus for this study was one group of middle management women matched as nearly as possible in background, education and early career experience to the group of twenty-five, but with the difference that they had chosen to give up their careers at or near the point of marriage. When asked why, they said that marriage and work were not possible at the same time, and that although they had known this when they left college, they had nonetheless thought they would "give it a try." When they found that they could not, as one woman said, "place their allegiance in two different places," they abandoned their careers.

In the light of this, one is left to wonder whether the process of managing the dual roles and responsibilities of wife-mother and career woman can ever be as simple as Barnett's Internalizers believed it to be. How *does* a woman begin to cope with the conflict between femininity and career achievement in her mid-twenties as against her mid-thirties? Is integration of the two issues even feasible initially?

The price paid for integration necessarily depends on the relationship between husband and wife and it is generally high because of the paradox that integration does not in fact take place. A woman typically has to be, and drives herself to be, both wife-mother *and* a woman with a serious career. She is the woman who works all day and comes home to prepare a dinner party for ten. She is the woman who works all day and assumes an extra burden of guilt if something happens to a child when she isn't there to prevent it or cope with it. She is the woman who must manage not just dual roles, but dual sets of anxieties each of which compounds the difficulties of the other. These conditions exist today. They were even more marked in the thirties when the twenty-five set out to work.

The twenty-five were not the idealized Internalizers of Barnett's study. They were much closer to the "confused" Identifiers who saw only one major commitment of their energies as being possible at any one time. They made their decisions, set their priorities and however simply, established plans for themselves and stuck to them—deferring gratification on one set of issues in order to find it in another. In contrast, Barnett's Internalizers were setting themselves up for the nearly impossible task of trying to balance too much too soon. The first decade of a management career is critically important—it is a decade of learning, of sorting out specific strengths and of finding the opportunity and the support to use them. It is hard and demanding work and however harsh it sounds the woman who enters a management career and decides to have children more or less simultaneously is setting herself a difficult task—a task that is almost unmanageable. And it is beside the point to say that men don't have to deal with this issue. The point is that women do.

The group of twenty-five decided to defer the issue. In their senior year in college, all of them made concrete plans for their careers after graduation. Most of them were graduating during the peak of the Depression and employment opportunities were almost nonexistent. While a limited number of graduate programs were open to women (almost no graduate professional schools wanted women), none of them considered graduate school immediately after college. One woman explained why:

"I was ready for action and felt that school had given me all I could get. I wanted to get out into the real world of business and show what I could do. I had gone the educational route and as far as I was concerned, I had beaten it and needed new and bigger challenges. I was scared as hell about finding a job, yet I couldn't live with the idea of not having one. I had been getting ready for that day as long as I could remember. It was a really tough time for me. It meant facing now, for real, all the things which I had convinced myself I was prepared to handle—both the task and the social things."

9

The First Career Decade

Despite the Depression all of the twenty-five found jobs. Twenty-three of them began as secretaries in business and financial institutions. One took a position as an administrative assistant and the other as an assistant buyer in a retail firm. Almost all of them got their jobs because of their fathers' connections or through friends of the family, and in most cases the job was specially created as a favor to the father or friend. Their starting salaries averaged $20 per week, and their initial responsibilities were limited. Several of them had to enroll in a secretarial school during the summer to learn typing and shorthand. All but two of the jobs were in New York City, which appeared to them to offer the best opportunity and the least resistance to career-oriented women.

The women's reactions to their first jobs varied, but they agreed that they felt fortunate to have a job at all when so many men were out of work. It was a first job and in their eyes, an enormous opportunity. They had a foot in the door and they thought they would have a chance to prove what they could do—and more, they would learn. None of them could recall thinking of or even wanting an "ideal" place to work. To start with it was enough that they should be accepted.

Several of the women changed jobs in the first two years because their original companies refused to accept women in anything but the most routine kinds of work and by the end of the third year none had achieved a change in job title. The companies for which they worked were in light and heavy manufacturing, consumer goods, retailing, banking, public relations, finance, insurance, the chemical industry and consulting and they all worked directly for, and were responsible to, lower-level male executives.

For the next thirty years none of the women worked for any other firm. One woman summarized what most of them said about this:

> "In the first year that I worked, I moved from my original employer to this company. After I worked here for a while, I decided that this was a good company. The people were decent and competent. I liked the kind of work they did, and I had a hell of a good boss. It was my decision then and there to stick with the company and my boss because I'd never have any better place to prove whether I had it or not. I decided that if I stayed in one place, I'd be able to learn this company—its business and its bosses—inside and out and this would be very important for me to master if I was going to have time to really excel at my work and get the kind of support I needed from my bosses."

This approach is less than typical of a highly motivated success-oriented male manager. Such a man is on the watch for every reasonable opportunity to get ahead and he regularly moves up the executive ladder through company changes. These women decided early in their careers to make it or break it in one company and their explanations of why they did so were uniform. They said that they had decided very early that a woman could move upward through the ranks of management only if she were more competent at her current job, at the job above her and at the job below her than any man available. This took enormous amounts of energy and concentration. They had also concluded that it was a great deal more difficult for a woman to establish good working relationships than it was for a man, and that once a woman had established those relationships it was an unproductive waste for her to move to another company and have to develop them all over again. The twenty-five did not believe that they were aware of precisely what one did to establish those relationships, but they were painfully aware that they needed all the energy they had to excel at their jobs and lacked both time and strength to cope with interpersonal relations that were constantly in flux. These were their initial reasons for the very choice of a career in a single company. As their careers developed, other reasons developed with them.

During their first ten years at work the twenty-five adopted an explicit strategy: it lay in knowing the company, its business and its people inside and out; in giving whatever time was necessary to establishing solid working relationships with the people around them; and above all in excelling at their job level. All of them saw their early job assignments as first steps leadng upward. In fact, one woman said that if she had thought of any of her first three jobs as terminal positions, she would have abandoned any thought of a career. Yet none of them could recall ever thinking of themselves as future presidents of their companies. They saw themselves as achieving responsible middle management positions, and at the time that seemed more than enough.

It was enough in the sense that they *were* thinking of the future and it helped them live with the frustrations of the day. They had already identified a critical make or break factor, the good boss. They had made explicit the need to understand the environments in which they worked, and they had committed themselves to excelling at what they did. They thought of themselves as competent and increasingly technically skilled, they felt themselves capable of establishing productive *working* relationships with superiors, peers and subordinates almost all of whom were men.

Acutely aware of their role as women in men's organizations and of the need to establish themselves within that context as they moved from the lower organizational levels where women predominated to middle management where they became the only women employed, they believed that success in achieving working relationships with men was based on keeping the issue of sexual difference to a minimum and ensuring that communication centered on the job or the task.

In short, they had found a place to work in which they were generally respected by others for their skills and abilities, where they were able to develop supportive work-centered relationships with others and where as a consequence they believed they had successfully mastered the environment. Even more important, because of their concentration on the work to be done and their own confidence that they could do it they were receiving very few negative signals about being a woman. They deliberately sought to minimize the possibility of this happening by seeking to establish relationships based on task and competence, and allowing any closer ties to develop solely on that basis. They low-keyed who they were and used competence as their primary definition of themselves. This both allowed and compelled the men around to deal with them on the most objective basis available— their own individual capacity, a basis which they controlled. It permitted men to say quite legitmately: "In spite of the fact she's a woman she's terribly good at her job—and I can and will and need to benefit from working with her." By then, as one woman put it, the company had become their harbor and their home.

What was happening to them in the world outside of work was quite different. They reported a steady decline in their social lives as they consciously chose to allot more and more of their time to their careers. One woman spoke for almost all:

"When I was twenty-six, I decided that I must choose between the kind of in-depth career I wanted and the idea of marriage in the next few years. I knew I could not do both, for to pursue my idea of a career I would need total freedom from other practical commitments. I would need all of my time available for work. I was more sympathetic now to women who tried to keep families going *and* a career. To have less of a career than I wanted was nothing to me. So the choice was really either-or. I chose to stick with the career and worry about marriage later. I figured that I was young and had plenty of time. I knew I could never give my all to that unless the career thing got worked through. I knew that I might well be giving up marriage forever by that choice, because there aren't that many eligible bachelors of any type around waiting for women of thirty-five who decide they now have time for marriage. I had all the relationships with men that I wanted right then at work, and I reasoned that that would have to be enough for the present."

Most of the women recalled making similar decisions at roughly the same age. None of them did marry until they were at least thirty-five years old and they said that in the ten years prior to age thirty-five, there was hardly any time to devote to personal relationships, vacations or even visiting their families. Few maintained any long-term relationship with men outside of work. Most had only one or two close women friends, usually sisters or other relatives.

Their either-or decision was less dramatic than realistic. The commitment expected and required by corporations of a person who wants to be marked for success in the first decade of a management career has traditionally been met by a young man who brings with him prior education and training, who accepts that his career will come first and that his wife and family will fit around it, who is willing to work as many hours as the job demands, who can travel out of town at short notice—and who must have a wife to manage every aspect of his life at home. The committed young woman competes with this young man during the first career decade and to compete successfully in the 1940s she had to more than match him step by step. She had to be better. Even more committed. She had to earn the phrase: "In spite of the fact she's a woman, she is so extraordinarily competent, efficient, effective, motivated." The costs were high. And they still are.

All of the women made it very clear that at no time during this period did they develop a sexual relationship with any of their business associates. Some said that they were too exhausted after work to find the energy. Several said that they had already learned an important lesson about sex and work: "Never say yes, never say no, always say maybe."

They believed that with some notable exceptions men viewed women basically as sexual objects, and as a result they believed it was important in maintaining their relationships that sex appeared not to be entirely ruled out—it was just difficult. They thought that if they did allow a sexual relationship to develop the word would spread and the man would inevitably become guilty over it and would reject them. On the other hand, they feared that if they made it immediately clear a sexual relationship was out of the question the man would reject them as being unfeminine.

Yet few of them reported being able over time to maintain successful "maybe" relationships and they recalled that their efforts were inordinately time-consuming and led to feelings of real conflict. They tried instead to avoid the issue entirely, basing their relationships on the job to be done, ignoring the innuendoes, double meanings and barely disguised propositions, trying not to care very much about how they were regarded.

In contrast, a deep and abiding friendship developed with the man for whom they worked. Without exception they began as his secretary or administrative assistant and as he moved upward in the organization they moved with him, always at his request. During their first ten years all of the women moved in this way to progressively higher positions in lower and middle management and an explicit understanding eventually developed between them that the woman would move upward with him through the company.

When asked to describe their boss and their relationship with him the women likened him to their fathers and described their relationship with him in similar terms. To each woman, he was her supporter, her encourager, her teacher and her strength in the company. He admitted her competence and her will to succeed. She in turn was his student, his admirer and his helper. He believed that women should be in business and backed up this belief in his dealings with her, with other men in the company and with male customers and clients. One woman described this vividly:

"As my boss and I progressed in the company, it became increasingly necessary for me to supervise men and to handle accounts which meant working with men clients from other firms. My first reaction to this requirement was that I could do okay with the male subordinates, but I thought I should stay away from direct contact with the clients. I was afraid most male clients were not ready to deal in confidence with a woman. When my boss heard this, he blew his stack. I remember that he screamed at me that it was the damnedest time for me to have an identity crisis. What he did was amazing to me: he went out to see every client we had and told them they would be working with me. He told them that I was the most skilled and able publicist in the company and they would be damn lucky if their account happened to be placed in my charge. Before I knew what was happening, our clients were actually asking for me, and I was getting more accounts than I and my group could handle. Over the years, I have developed long and close friendships with a number of my male clients, many of whom are now chief executives of their respective firms. I never did have any real trouble with clients. New clients were sometimes reserved, but after I talked with them for a while they became aware of the other accounts that I was managing and for how long I had been doing so. Regardless of what they felt about my being a woman, they knew I knew my trade. I really have to thank Jim [the boss] for all of my success. My dad got me to college and Jim took me from there."

This statement captures the feeling and much of the content of the recollections of all of the twenty-five. The boss acted as sales agent for the woman wherever he sent her, both inside and outside of the company. He used his reputation to develop hers, and his respect from others to gain acceptance for her. In times of direct confrontation with any group or individual, he would act as a buffer and place himself between the woman and her opponent. He was the protector and she the protected. His support helped provide her with the extra confidence she needed to take on new responsibilities, new tests of her competence and new positions. He reinforced her own emphasis on competence as the issue of paramount importance.

The women were immeasurably sustained by this relationship. It gave them the base they needed to acquire new and much broader skills and they did so in the certainty that it was worth doing. They continued their education in selective ways, concentrating on the acquisition of new technical skills—a woman in accounting, for example, took further courses in tax law. None of them registered for standard graduate programs; instead they selected courses which they saw as contributing quickly and directly to improving their competence at and beyond a given job level.

Their strategy was to achieve mastery of a given

job's tasks and requirements, and having done so (they could now do that job "with one hand tied behind their back"), to prepare for the next job up the line by studying at home and attending school at night. By the end of their term in every job they held, they had overqualified themselves to continue in it and they were already capable of filling a position at the next level up. When their boss was promoted, they were ready to move.

By their early thirties the women were supervising and managing male subordinates. They faced almost identical problems and they devised very similar strategies. One woman's description was typical:

"As soon as I began getting male subordinates, I had to examine the situation and decide how I was going to handle it. Until then my managing of people had been limited to typists and researchers. Now I was going to have to learn to manage in the real sense of the word. First, I had to accept that most men would not like to work for a woman, and I was a woman. Second, I had to accept that I had developed a style of being dependent upon my boss for support which I could not do with subordinates. Next, I had to realize that they were probably not going to be dependent upon me. Given all of this, I had to decide what I wanted from them and what they could possibly hope to get from me. I determined it was learning and skill. I wanted them to develop it and use it and if they wanted to get ahead, they wanted this, too. If they respected my skills, they might want to become as skilled, and hence move ahead in their careers. I concluded that the thing to do was to try and overlook the man-woman thing and concentrate on making my department the kind of training group that has a reputation for being the place where men can come, learn and get a good promotion. This was my way of getting men to want to work for me. This worked very well, and I never did deal with the man-woman thing but rather I tried to compensate for it in advance."

Technical skill and competence were the linchpins of these women's success in the first career decade and their effectiveness on the job was increasingly matched by their ability to use their own competence as a means of controlling interpersonal relationships—not simply defensively, but more and more as a deliberate, conscious means of managing men. It meant thinking through situations, assessing needs and wants, anticipating possible outcomes and developing a style for the supervision of subordinates quite different from the style they had established with their own bosses. Certainly this was happening at a career point when a subordinate's skills are highly important to a senior manager; if *he* wants to move ahead then he must surround himself with people who can contribute to his job achievement. Equally, the subordinates of these women-in-the-middle would have tended at this point to be new, young and motivated to learn in order to move ahead in their careers. Yet the difference was that they *were* women, and to superiors as well as to subordinates, as women they needed to demonstrate not just a higher degree of technical competence than the going average, but that they were worth working for and thus capable of managing others and thus promotable to still higher levels of responsibility.

With their male peers, however, the twenty-five had few contacts and their relationships with even the few tended to be work-centered. Communication was limited to the only common ground they felt was shared, work and the job. They translated their thoughts into male terms. They talked shop and they sought to act in ways which would obscure the fact that they were women. One woman described what this meant:

"The strategy with most of the men who had to be dealt with but didn't know you well was to remain unnoticed as a woman but very visible as a highly skilled task specialist. This was very hard to do, and when you had to work with these guys you tried to be just that—one of the guys. It was terribly important not to do anything that might leave yourself open to being accused of acting like a woman. You dressed carefully and quietly to avoid attracting attention; you had to remember to swear once in a while, to know a few dirty jokes and never to cry if you got attacked. You fended off all attempts of men to treat you like a woman; you opened the doors before they could hold them, sat down before a chair could be held and threw on a coat before it could be held for you. You wanted to be desired because you were skilled, not because you were a woman. In spite of all this extra work you still couldn't be sure, if a guy seemed to warm up to you, whether it was the skill or the woman he was after. It was terribly easy to turn off anybody who was warm because you couldn't really trust his motives, and by God, you only wanted recognition for your job!"

The problems and the pain of dealing with the "threat" of sexual involvement may seem clear in this statement. Yet, if as these women believed, most men saw them first as essentially sexual objects and their intelligence and capacity as only a distant second, then "turning off anybody who was warm" had less to do with sexual threat than it did with intellectual threat. And they were intellectually threatened when they saw their concept of themselves *as women who were successful managers* threatened. It was an issue they had pushed to an extreme and they did so searching for clarity in the perpetual ambiguity of "Is it the skill or the woman he is after?" If it turned out to be "the woman" what did her skills represent? Nothing? What did the price she had paid to acquire them matter? Nothing? If she allowed a sexual relationship to develop could she be sure that she was valued for anything more than simply being a woman? She valued her own skills and abilities. She was painfully uncertain that her male peers did and she sacrificed confirmation as a woman in order to be certain of confirmation as a manager.

Only with their bosses, as with their fathers earlier, did they feel confident that their gender was taken for granted and primary emphasis placed on their intelligence and ability. During the first career decade the behavioral style these women adopted with their peers was as a consequence direct, factual, business- and task-oriented and emotionally distant. Close social relationships were discouraged and although all of them referred to at least one man at the same management level with whom they developed a warm friendship, when they described what it was like they said he took them home to the wife and kids.

As the twenty-five moved upward their administrative responsibilities broadened. They continued to deal with the men around them on the basis of the work to be done and how well it was done and they saw the functions of higher management as simply demanding deeper technical knowledge and skill. As they began to realize that they could acquire both their aspirations changed. Where earlier they believed that a middle management position would be their ultimate achievement, they now began to think of themselves as capable of reaching more senior executive positions. They said that they began to feel "successful" in ways they had been afraid to think about before. They sensed that they were securely established in their companies, for life if they wanted it, and they believed for the first time that they could always do at least as well as they were then doing. Entirely self-confident at the technical levels of their companies' work they began to look more closely at the technical requirements of higher positions in their firms. Many of them said that at about this time their relationship with their boss began to change. They had become more autonomous and less personally dependent upon him and the relationship itself had begun to assume an increasing degree of equality. He was less protective and they gave him less reason to be.

By the end of this first decade, they had all moved into positions of considerable responsibility and they found satisfaction and reward in their work. But it was a period in which they had committed their lives to their jobs and had let social contacts dwindle to nearly nothing. Within the work environment, they were close to their bosses, and they worked comfortably with clients, customers and subordinates who reinforced their concept of themselves as superior task specialists.

It was a period in which they had sought very carefully for reinforcement of their concept of themselves and had consciously avoided confronting sexual problems or issues. They had eliminated these from their social lives, avoided involvement with the majority of their peers at work and identified only a very few non-threatening work relationships as being personally relevant. By acting in this way they avoided having to come to grips with themselves as women. They did not attempt to deny that they were women, rather they avoided any confrontation with the reality that they were, because this might have affected their ability to live with the priorities they had set for themselves.

They believed that at this point in their careers their male associates at work considered them to be serious, highly skilled, work-oriented and certainly ambitious. They had no clear idea whether they were thought of as "nice people" but they were aware that they were often responded to as if they were cold and reserved. Yet all of them said that their bosses, and in some cases their customers and clients, responded to them as warm and human people, which was how they wanted to regard themselves.

They approached the midpoint of their careers in positions of growing responsibility. Their aspirations rose. Yet they saw themselves, despite their awareness of the changing nature of their relationships with their bosses, as simply more successful versions of their earlier task-oriented selves.

10

Career Maturity

A clear difference emerged among the five subsidiary groups of women who formed part of this study in the ways in which they talked about themselves, their careers and the relationship they saw between the two.* For four of the groups (women who had given up their careers in middle management, but who were similar in age and background to the twenty-five; women still in middle management positions; M.B.A. graduates; and undergraduates majoring in business administration) the management of career and marriage was a question that could be dealt with in only one way: they believed that a woman needed to be a man at work and a woman at home.

In contrast, the fifth group of higher-level women executives (the ten women in the pilot survey who were not included in the group of twenty-five because of their location off the eastern seaboard) admitted having held similar beliefs in the first ten years of

---

* See pp. 87-91.

their careers. And then they talked of having deliberately chosen a major new direction which led them to adjust work and non-work behavior in ways which brought both closer together, made them more congruent and released more energy for life in general.

By the end of *their* first ten years the twenty-five had established an identity, part of which critically depended upon their avoidance of conflicts arising over the fact of their sex. Facing up to conflict of this kind would have compelled them to cope with the discrepancies which existed between their own concepts of themselves and others' definitions of the roles of women. This pattern of avoidance heavily influenced their behavioral style, leading them to withdraw from relationships with most of the men and women they knew. It was a pattern which in one form or another they had relied on from childhood—a pattern which served to keep intact their own concepts of themselves. Their most important sources of confirmation were first their fathers and then their bosses. The special blessing of these all-important men helped them defend against conflict, let them see themselves as women and confirmed their own belief that the acquisition of competence was an essential part of life. They did not consciously deny their sexual identity—they simply refused to engage it. At about the age of twenty-five, all of them, as one of them said, "had taken their femininity and stored it away for future consideration." Their objectives were achievement, success, recognition. They achieved, they succeeded and they were recognized. It was a cycle which endlessly reconfirmed the rightness of the choices they had made.

By their mid to late thirties, the twenty-five had moved up to positions in the higher levels of middle management and at this point a number of factors which had previously held constant began to change.

Their fathers had grown older, become less alert and in a number of cases senility or death occurred. Their previously close relationships with their bosses underwent major change and they experienced a marked increase in autonomy on the job. In the process their perception of what they had achieved shifted radically. One woman said:

"Until I reached upper middle management, my philosophy about being a woman was to make that fact as unnoticeable as possible. This applied to me as well as all others. My personal style was to be business-like and that meant being an enlightened genteel *man* in style of behavior. I dressed in as unprovocative a way as possible; I was a suits and tailored dresses type, always rejecting frills and pink. As far as emotions were concerned, I was convinced that nothing would turn a man off more than an emotional woman, and I drove myself to be as coldly rational and logical as possible in all my dealings with men. I often fought my own emotions but never let that become visible to others. Then a number of things happened to me. I began to be aware of the fact that I no longer needed to try so hard with those I worked with. I felt more secure in my job than I ever had before. I think this let me relax a little, something which I almost didn't know how to do. I also realized that I was not depending on my dad as much as before; in fact, my parents were now depending on me and he would call me for advice.

"Most of all, I think I began to find my job less rewarding and challenging. I began to realize that I was getting older and had very little in life other than that job. There were few skills that I hadn't mastered and my job was not challenging me at that level. I couldn't really get any better at it than I was. My boss was now several slots up in corporate administration, while I was still heading a department. We were seeing each other less and less, and he was having very little to do with me directly in my present position.

"I had really reached a plateau in my career and for the present it wasn't exciting me. I knew something had to be done. I think, unconsciously at first, I was really concerned about being an unmarried woman reaching middle age too. I had always been able to avoid that one because I always saw myself as young with plenty of time to devote to that later—when I got the career under control. But there I was at thirty-five; time had crept up on me and I worried about things like not being able to have children much longer. Life wasn't as exciting at work and life outside of work was virtually non-existent."

Statements by the other women were similar in both content and feeling. For the first time in many years their lives at work and in the world outside demanded critical scrutiny. For the first time a preoccupation with femininity emerged. This was an issue which they had always been able to "put away until later." Now it became a dominant concern.

It was difficult to assess whether it was the "job plateau"—the sense of routine, the sameness, which contributed to their new awareness, or whether it was time itself. The probability was that the two worked together. They realized that with the passing of time, they could hardly afford to postpone until later still a reconsideration of the value to them of marriage and motherhood. And such a reconsideration was impossible without taking their work and its rewards and the entire direction of their lives into account:

"I finally had to face the fact that I wasn't married, I didn't have any children, and I damn well better decide now whether I wanted either. Time was finally calling me to task and I had to come to some decisions on issues which I had put off for years. Way back when I first started, I had convinced myself to put off marriage for a time so I could give all of myself to my career. But I was still young then and questions of biological age were not important. Then, suddenly, the few years were twelve years and I was thirty-six. I had already achieved what I had set out to do, and then found I was faced with the same decisions I had to face at twenty-four. Only now it was a crisis situation. I was smart enough to know that going on to try to achieve top management would be as different as night and day from my previous jobs and might well be just as time- and life-consuming as my previous career. I seemed to be much less sure of the relationship between marriage and career for me than I was ten years ago.

"I saw three possibilities: marry and quit; marry and stay at my same position; or not marry and go forth on my next career stage. I knew that there was a fourth alternative—find a very unique type of man to marry who would be willing to go along with the time and personal investment of having a career-striving wife—but I figured I would never be unique enough to make a go of such a marriage if I could find such a rare fellow. No matter how I looked at it, I still had to decide on marry or not marry first. Somehow that seemed to come before the career.

"I decided I needed time—something I had not had in years. So I decided to let the career ride for a year or so to see what I could do about my personal and social life. Somehow I felt just like an adolescent again, starting out to achieve my first dates. I figured the question of having kids had better follow finding the husband, and I was not at all adverse to adoption or taking on a widower's family. I did know that I'd never be happy just staying at home all day so I figured that at least I'd hang on to my present position."

This woman came to the clear conclusion that a moratorium on career striving should be declared. She needed time to reassess her personal life, its present limited goals and its possible future satisfactions. It was a strategy that was to be followed by every one of the women and for identical reasons.

There was no doubt that they had left major aspects of their identities in abeyance to this point. Biological time and career time had both caught up with them, precipitating a crisis which left them willing to reopen the unresolved issues their drive to achieve and to succeed had obscured. These issues centered on their inability to integrate the fact of femininity and their career interests into a balanced, coherent whole. They had grown progressively less able to believe the message of their childhoods—that one could be a woman and much else besides, that one need not be limited by others' definitions of who one should and ought to be. As managers in the nineteen forties and fifties they had had to contend with companies whose cultures were rigidly masculine. As they repetitively became "the first woman who . . ." they sought to deal with the incongruity they felt in others and themselves by acting as if they were neither men nor women but rather extremely knowledgeable, superbly efficient and unusually rational automatons. Where in childhood and adolescence they had believed that a woman could be different—could be an achiever and still be a woman—the realities of their career lives had inevitably led them to believe and to act as if a woman could have one or the other—not both. The two issues had to be held separate or one would affect the other to its detriment.

The changes that now occurred were of major interest. The theme of either-or, the separation of achievement from *traditional* definitions of femininity, had been clear throughout their lives. Conflict within themselves and between themselves and others over the issues of femininity and achievement, of sex and career, had earlier been denied by virtue of self-concepts which allowed them to see themselves as "special," and different from the traditional woman. As the going got tougher, as their careers expanded and they came increasingly into competition with men, they found that however much they might feel they differed from traditional women, in many men's eyes *any* woman was still a woman—no more, no less. Only if a woman made herself appear as little like a woman as possible did she seem to have a chance. They felt this despite the unusual support their bosses gave them and they expressed it by deliberately de-emphasizing the feminine side of themselves and increasingly emphasizing the value to them of achievement.

The issue of femininity remained. To this point these women clearly felt that any commitment to resolving the conflict might so absorb them that they would risk losing all—both the promise of resolution and their careers. Now, with a greater sense of career security than they had ever felt before, they began to move toward resolution. While their individual experiences vary, the emotional dynamics and the eventual outcomes are consistent.

They all began by slowing their drive for immediate achievement. They made every attempt to free themselves at work. They refused extra responsibilities they would have seized on in the past, and they began to delegate current responsibilities and authority to subordinates where previously they had kept the tightest possible control. For the first time in their careers they found themselves with time on their hands and they used it in new ways. They literally "did themselves over." All of them spoke of buying new and feminine wardrobes and a number of them made appointments at expensive beauty salons—emerging with entirely new looks in hairstyles and make-up. They talked of reaching a decision to look and act like what they were —women. Their own ideas of an appropriate role for women did not change. What changed was their own view of themselves in the settings in which they worked.

They came to accept that they no longer needed to avoid the symbols which they and others identified with "traditional" women. They said that this became very important to them, because they felt it signified to others their own willingness to be viewed as women. Still more important, it committed them to engaging, rather than avoiding, conflicts arising over their own role choices and what others perceived as appropriate roles for women. As adolescents might do, they put on the uniforms of women first to convince themselves, and second to test the legitimacy of assumptions and perceptions based on accepted definitions of femininity others held.

They said that they re-established old social contacts, called friends from earlier days and began to build a life outside of work. Simultaneously their work relationships began to change. Included for the first time in their social lives were people with whom they worked. One woman said:

"I became an absolute social butterfly. For the second time in my life. The first time I did it because I was supposed to, and I had to—or so it seemed. This time I did it because I wanted to. I was very curious about myself in relation to other people—what I had become, what they had become. Don't misunderstand that I expected anything great. In fact, I wasn't convinced at all that I'd like it or that anything would come of it. I believed that I had to experience it in order to be able to make my own choices, and live with them. I viewed the choices that I would make now on things like career and marriage as partially irreversible and permanent for my future life, and I wanted to be darn sure that I knew what I was discarding for the rest of my life and what the relative costs were going to be."

Another woman said:

"When I decided to turn over my new leaf, I started with a new wardrobe and hairstyle. These were *things* and the easiest place to start. But the dynamics soon came to bear. I was really petrified about going to work with this new look. The first few days I got a lot of stares and double takes and some kidding and whistles from people who knew me better. Everyone seemed to look at me in a new way and so I did at myself and I liked the way it felt to be looked at that way. As time passed I began to respond to that new look. I think that for once, I could distinguish that those looks were specifically for me as a woman. I looked forward to being noticed, to being admired by men that way. Don't think I don't realize how egocentric this sounds; but remember for fifteen years I had cut myself off from this part of life entirely. It was fun again. Granted, it wore off after a while, but in that time I know that I changed forever. I learned to understand and accept and, yes, like and enjoy another very real part of me. I may have taken time and clothes and whistles to accomplish it, but I was a new and stronger person for it. Listening to myself talk now, I don't much like the person I used to be and it really sounds foolish—what it took to discover that I existed all by myself and that I liked that person and that others did too."

During the period of withdrawal and subsequent change, half of these women married. Those who did married widowers or divorced men, all of whom had children. The husbands were at least ten years older than their new wives, none of whom subsequently bore children of their own. Whether the rest of the women chose not to marry or whether the opportunity never arose, they remained open to the idea of marriage even in their fifties.

Those who did marry said that they decided jointly with their husbands to continue in their careers. Each of them believed her husband to be unique not only in his willingness to accept this kind of marriage, but in his drive to encourage her to move ahead in her career. They said that they thought their husbands were delighted to see them rise higher in their firms. They believed that their husbands loved and respected them as women for whom a career in no way clashed with femininity. Understandably enough the husbands all held secure professional positions and earned incomes that were then more than double the incomes of their wives.

All of the twenty-five worked through these fundamental changes in two years or less and then recommitted themselves to their careers. They now saw themselves as capable of moving toward the highest management levels in their firms and they talked about their ability to acknowledge this freely and openly, aware that they had come to understand themselves better as a result of having successfully changed the directions of their lives. They characterized this period as one in which they became whole people, a time when they came of age as mature adult women.

Clearly it was a period in which they finally came to terms with who they were. They were finally able to accept the fact of their sexual identity, not as "special" or "different," but even in others' terms as an essential part of the person they were, and to bring that identity and their careers together into a coherent whole. They no longer felt driven to prove that they were persons despite the disadvantage of having been born women. They *were* women. They *were* managers. And they were capable of being both. They took account of what they had become and they redefined where they wanted to go. Their redefinition represented no drastic change in the over-all direction of their careers; rather it had to do with self-acceptance and with a bringing into balance and perspective parts of themselves which they had previously kept carefully apart. They brought consciously together their personal and career autonomy, the degree of success they had already achieved, their reduced need for dependence on their families and their bosses and the promise which the future held for their careers. In doing so, they freed themselves to accept and deal with issues which previously had been shot through with conflict. The suppression of femininity which their earlier behavioral style had demanded was discarded. They now adopted a style which deliberately challenged others' acceptance of the traditional women's stereotype in that here they were, clearly and comfortably, women, acting in situations that were equally clearly beyond the scope of the stereotyped woman's role.

All of them said that their relationships at work became freer and more open. Where earlier they had devoted a great deal of energy to controlling and repressing themselves as women and to translating their perception of male styles into their own behavior, they now consciously abandoned these attempts at role-playing and began to let their own styles evolve. They said that they felt the greatest sense of relief and satisfaction in feeling free to do basically what was natural to them at any given time. One woman said that for the first time in her life she did not feel she had to plan her every word and action in advance. This, she said, did not mean that she was no longer conscious of words and feelings, but rather that she no longer felt compelled to deny what she felt or to translate herself to others as feeling other than she did. The results of these changes were apparently marked. One woman said:

"There seemed to be more time to do everything than before. I was doing a better job than before and people obviously liked me better at the same time. I began to realize that my goal at work had been to be something like a well-oiled machine running at top speed—nothing more human than that. Now that I had accepted myself I began to enjoy people as well as tasks. The whole heart of a manager's job seemed to come into perspective for me. It was a combination of task concern and people concern. I came across a book that I had on something called *The Managerial Grid*. I had thought in an earlier reading that it was bunk; now I took another look at it, and it really came across to me. I thought that now I could accomplish more and be happy about it too. I could do it."

In fact, they became increasingly aware that their own need to be what they felt they were resulted in their behaving toward others in ways which others perceived to be more honest and real, and there were many outcomes of this development. In their accounts of this period they consistently added the word "happy" to their descriptions of themselves, where previously they had used the words "rewarded" and "satisfied." They became aware of a new sense of self-acceptance, of a coherent, put-together self. They enjoyed the rediscovery of social skills they had long abandoned. They said that for the first time they felt able to discuss openly their earlier feelings about work and a career in relation to marriage. They felt free to talk about their new choices in ways which no longer left them with the uncomfortable feeling that somehow others saw them as diminished women for having chosen as they did. Several women summarized this by saying that obviously everyone around them knew that they were achievement-and success-oriented and they had now learned that it made others more comfortable to hear them say it about themselves. As they became more real to themselves, they evidently became more real in the eyes of their associates. As they felt freer to communicate with others, others felt freer to communicate with them.

Another interesting development during this period was a change in the rationalization underlying their attitudes toward other women. They reported that they were increasingly able to see that it was not even the "traditional woman" whom they disliked but rather that they disliked being with anyone with whom they had nothing in common. Where earlier they had been unwilling to hire or sponsor another, and possibly "traditional" woman because of their fear that she might challenge or upset the delicate behavioral balance they had established with the men with whom they worked, they now believed that they were less concerned about such a possibility and much more concerned about losing their unique "queen bee" status with their associates. They felt that they had finally achieved a different kind of specialness which they did not want to share, and they believed that "other women might become jealous" of what they had achieved. Almost all of them took this position and said that while they "were not happy" about it, they were unable to convince themselves that they should take on women managers as subordinates.

Over the next few years, all of them rose to the presidency or vice-presidency of their firms. By then their earlier bosses had either become board chairmen or presidents or in a few cases had retired. The relationship between them had become a relationship of equals. Many of the unmarried women described this relationship as a "working marriage" in which each party to the relationship was both dependent on and independent of the other.

The change in this relationship was yet another reflection of the changed way in which these women saw their jobs. Earlier, they had been almost entirely skill-

and task-oriented. They had been highly controlled and highly controlling in their job functions. They had seen little need for human skills in their jobs. During this period of personal change they began to delegate much of their routine work to others and to persuade rather than dominate their subordinates. They began to relate to their associates as people rather than as mere accomplishers of work, and as they became more behaviorally adept, they felt increasingly capable of moving beyond their current jobs. Their re-evaluation of themselves made them rethink their earlier perceptions of others and led them to recognize qualities and abilities which they had previously overlooked. They began to place emphasis on both human and technical skills. They developed a capacity to blend people with very different skills and abilities into effective working teams. And they agreed that while the question of marriage and the worrying pressures of age were the immediately conscious crises which precipitated this period of profound personal change, in the end the result had less to do with their own growth and development than with their need to reach out to find a comfortable, acceptable sense of themselves.

In comparing the final period of these women's careers with the group of women who remained at the middle management level, the major difference between them lay in the occurrence of the moratorium. For the group of twenty-five, this was a time of self-assessment, of re-evaluation, of personal risk-taking. It enabled them to make the transition from middle to upper management because they freed themselves to acquire new personal and organizational skills. The women who remained in middle management underwent no such experience and they remained primarily task- and skill-oriented. They clung to self-concepts and behavioral styles which were masculine in orientation, and they possessed few human skills to bring to bear on their work. In short, this group of women continued to accept that their sexual identity and their careers were necessarily in conflict and they sought to cope with that conflict by evading the fact of femininity. They maintained and strengthened further a behavioral style which sought to deny that they were women. Rather than work themselves through it, they made themselves over in its image. They felt bitter toward men who had stood in their way and impeded their rise to higher positions. They reported feeling frustrated and cheated. The majority were unmarried and they felt they had made a mistake in giving up marriage since it could have saved them from their present unhappy situation. They saw themselves as cold and domineering people who had been forced by painful experience to become what they were. They generally disliked other women whose "typical women's behavior" they saw as hampering the career woman's ability to get ahead.

The difference between the two groups lay in the degree of self-knowledge, understanding and acceptance which the members of each possessed. The twenty-five were able to grow and develop as individuals as well as managers, while the others were frustrated at both levels. The twenty-five reported a sense of satisfaction and congruence, while the middle management women reported feeling closed, bitter, defensive, unhappy and frozen in their present jobs. They were, in fact, stuck at the mid-career stage.

Some of the other marked differences between the two groups was the way in which they dealt with the feeling of loss associated with the years of concentration on their careers and its emotional cost. The twenty-five made a conscious and systematic effort to deal with the sense of loss. They did not attempt to

make emotional scapegoats of their organizations, of
the men with whom they worked or of other women,
as did the middle management comparison group.
They were able to face the costs to themselves openly,
as primarily the consequence of their own decisions
and their own acts. They had experienced enough
conflict in their attempts to deal with the questions of
marriage, motherhood, friendship and the issue of being a women that for most of them unhappiness and
even depression had ensued accompanied by a
marked loss of interest in their jobs. All of these issues
combined to precipitate the personal crisis which
drove each of them into a moratorium on career
achievement and into reassessment of their lives.
There is no way to know how much inner conflict they
found themselves compelled to deal with. Certainly
the relaxation of tension and the sense of freedom that
followed the moratorium suggest that considerable
energy had gone into managing it.

The difficult and enticing question which cannot be
clearly answered is why one group of women was able
to recognize the need for reassessment and re-
evaluation while the other was not.

Part of the answer almost certainly lies in the nature of the organizations in which these women
worked and the ways in which the men with whom
they worked were able to offer support, respect and
security.

But the greater part of the answer perhaps lies in
the deeper experiences of their childhood which provided the twenty-five with so much inner strength.
One recalls the woman who said that her family was
so secure that each member dared venture out and
take risks because no matter what happened they
would all come together again. From their families,
and more especially from their fathers, they had

gained the certain knowledge that women did not need to be men in order to be persons. In mid-life they were finally able to act on what they had always known.

The twenty-five women frozen in middle management came from families in which the parent-child relationships differed essentially. Their fathers, acting toward them as if they *were* sons, had effectively intensified the daughters' sense of conflict over being a woman and succeeding in a man's career. The fathers' message to their daughters had been that they needed to be a man to succeed. Their femininity initially denied, some of them even bearing boys' names, these women moved into their first jobs and then into the lower levels of management with a "buddy" style which sought desperately to establish their credentials as "one of the boys." The problem was that the boys ultimately left them behind, and with their style set, these women went on to repeat with successive groups of younger and still younger peers the only pattern of relationships they knew. Left behind in middle management, unwilling or unable to think through what they might themselves have contributed to their own condition, their bitterness and resentment became focused on the people "who had done it to them." The mid-thirties crisis which the successful twenty-five worked through evaded them entirely. In their own minds they saw themselves as in a state of ongoing crisis which was not of their own making, for which they were not responsible and upon which they could not and would not act.

Their concepts of themselves and the styles of behavior which emerged out of their self-concepts denied that they were women and it was a conflict only too readily visible. However hard they tried, the image they projected was far distant from the male corporate norm, which, demanding as it does a great deal from men, does so against a background of shared aspiration and expectation, on the basis of a common set of assumptions, of readily understood styles of behavior. The women frozen at the middle management level sought to fit that norm—and failed. The twenty-five sought finally to change it—and succeeded.

PART III

11

What Women Can Do

In this chapter we come face to face with the critical issue: it is that many women currently in management jobs or anticipating management careers are affected on the one hand by the patterns of difference we discussed in Part I, and on the other cannot possibly have brought with them to adulthood the unique array of strengths which so clearly contributed to the career achievements of the twenty-five.

Given that we cannot change our birth order, that we cannot redo our families or rework our early relationships, that we cannot reverse time or alter past events, can a woman who does not share the advantages the twenty-five shared nonetheless learn to deal successfully with the problematic differences in assumption, perception and behavior we discussed in Part I?

We believe she can. We know it won't be easy. We are certain it will take time and a great deal of effort. But we also know that it can be done because we have seen it done.

The first step lies in accepting that the residues of difference will remain with us for the rest of our lives. A woman may always be anxious over the potential conflict between being a high achiever and a successful woman. She may always be vulnerable to criticism in a way that is more directly personal than it is for men. She may always see career risk as a little more dangerous. She may always find it difficult to be aggressive and to initiate in her own cause. These residues will remain. They need to be identified and managed. Situations which bring them back in strength need to be anticipated and planned for and one needs to practice at the lower end of the scale so that gradations can be consciously established in what represents conflict, vulnerability, risk, aggressiveness.

The second step is the most critical of all. It is the decision whether one really wants to succeed in a management career, a career that requires competing primarily with men, and competing with them in a system they understand better and on terms with which they are far more comfortable and much more familiar.

Traditionally, women have had great difficulty in making a decision as to whether they want a career and just as much difficulty in planning how to go about it. The concepts and the tools needed to evaluate the true costs and rewards for them as women have been left out of most career planning exercises. Unable to analyze where they came from, what they brought with them and where they were going, women have been able to do little about where they were.

However roughly they do it, and many do it with considerable care and perception, men develop and implement action plans for their careers while women have tended to store away feelings about the lack of movement in theirs. Plans can be implemented, tested, modified and even abandoned. Feelings tend to stay where they are.

A woman must be able to say with confidence that she wants a career and that she is willing to confront the problems she will inevitably encounter. She must be willing to be far more specific in her planning than the men around her and even more alert at anticipating situations which might accentuate the pressure she will feel or expose the vulnerabilities she will continue to sense. She must in other words be clear on the need to manage her environment and herself concurrently.

This does not mean changing who she is. She will alter the outcomes of her life at work less by trying to change her personality and much more by effectively managing the interaction between who she is and the environment in which she must work. The likelihood that one can or would want to rid oneself of all the vestiges of one's upbringing is small. The likelihood that one can learn to manage one's personality far more effectively is great. The fundamental question is, do you want to? And if so, how much?

This leads into a second set of questions. What are the costs and what are the rewards of a management career? Is the balance positive? Are you sure? If the answer is a serious yes, recognize that this is the answer most men have often explicitly decided on before they enter an M.B.A. program, or when at twenty-two they enter a management training program as a first step to their first job. Because it is an answer typically reached against a background of much greater difficulty, a woman needs to be that much clearer about what will be involved. The process of clarification begins with a further series of questions most women have probably never asked themselves before: Do I expect to be working for most of my life? Do I expect to work regardless of what else I may do? Whether or not I marry, whether or not I have children? If I expect to work over the long term what do I want out of it? What do I really want to achieve? Where do I want to be five years, ten years, twenty years from now?

One can most usefully begin at a point two or three years away with a number of critically important questions: What kind of job do I want to be in by then? Where is it? What do I need to know to be able to do it? What level of experience does it require? What kind of knowledge base? What are the skills needed? At what level of competence? What kinds of relationships will be important in getting it? Who are these people?

Returning to the present, another series of questions needs to be answered: Where am I now? What is my present level of knowledge, skill and competence? Who are the people I know? What positions do they hold? What can they help me with? What can they teach me? What information do they have that I need? Whom do they know who can help me?

Be as specific as you can for you must be able to assess prior experience, prior achievement in ways which allow you to measure your own potential. Many women, automatically, without thinking, discount what they have done. Every new job brings that sinking feeling of having to start all over again. Deal with this deliberately. Force yourself to go through every job you have held. Break down each job in terms of what you learned—new knowledge, new skills you developed or old ones you enhanced—assess how effective you were in applying those skills—the level of competence you achieved. If you find this process difficult then identify specific incidents, crises, tests that you had to deal with and dealt with successfully in the course of the job. How did you do it? What were the skills involved—technical and behavioral? Repeat this process for every job you have held and then look at the list. It will spell out what you know, what you can do and how well you can do it.

This process is vital for women in their forties who have been in and out of the job market over a period of years. It is even more so for women whose entire work experience has been with volunteer organizations. We found a striking example of the "discounting of prior experience" phenomenon in the career history of a housewife in the Midwest who had simultaneously held leadership positions at the local and national level in a number of volunteer organizations. She had done this for twenty years. In the course of it she had managed seven-figure budgets. She had raised funds in large amounts. She had chaired policy committees. She had managed organizations of both paid and volunteer personnel. In the twentieth year her husband fell seriously ill and she was forced to find a paying job. She panicked. She could think of nothing she was qualified to do. Finally she decided she would get a job as a cab driver. The only skills she could determine she had were that she drove well and knew every street in the city. Fortunately for her a man with whom she had worked on fund-raising projects was president of a large local bank. At a board meeting for one of their projects she told him about her need for a paid job and she discussed the process by which she had arrived at her decision to drive a cab. He was appalled. He told her that she had more useful experience than the average vice-president in his bank. He offered her a job—he opened up the bank's eighteen-month management training program to her (she was fifty years old). She completed the program in eight months and joined the bank's executive staff as vice-president for public relations.

This incident is much less than typical in its successful outcome because so many women with extensive management experience in volunteer organizations never think of evaluating what they've done. If you are such a woman and you don't know how to begin the process of evaluation then look for help. Contact a division of continuing education at a local college or a faculty member in the department of management. Find a women's counseling center or a vocational training group. Enroll in a life accreditation seminar. Many women's colleges are now running these seminars specifically to teach women how to go about translating and accrediting their unpaid work experiences. And most important, don't forget that the senior managers with whom you've worked on volunteer projects are also the employers of thousands of paid employees. You know them, they know you. Use these friendships as important sources of help and support.

Once you have identified what you have done and what you can do as specifically as possible, the process of filling in the space between where you are and where you want to go begins. On the average the individual woman has more to manage than a male counterpart and many things to make up as well. A plan that will be effective in getting her from where she is to where she wants to go must be specific and very detailed. She must define each of the steps in between: *What* jobs must be held between now and then? *How* does she get them and *when*? *Who* will help? What will she have to learn? How is she going to learn it? Who can help her learn it? She must cite job requirements, positions, experimental learning, training courses and above all the people who will necessarily be involved. To whom can she take this plan to get realistic feedback? Is her boss the person? Does she know anyone else who might help? Is there another woman whose boss seems more helpful and supportive?

At this stage she has to begin to look for a coach, a godfather or godmother, a mentor, an advocate, someone in a more senior management position who can teach her, support her, advise her, critique her. To succeed in this she must present herself as someone worth investing in, as someone who can make a return on the help she receives. Then, having done all of this she must estimate what it will really take to do it. Is the plan realistic in terms of her total time commitments? Can she make it more realistic? Will it be rewarding enough to cover the personal costs she will have to pay?

The approach we are suggesting makes a tangible difference. It helps a woman move toward a position from which she can begin to control her career life. She becomes more active, less reactive. The process of evaluating whether or not she has a career leads to an identification of the kind of career she wants and what it is going to take to achieve it. If she does this realistically and objectively she can decide whether or not it's worth it, and even if her decision is that it is not, she benefits from having taken control of where she's going. Knowing for certain that she doesn't want a career frees her to make other choices. One woman we know was finally able to see that her real goal was to save enough to buy a house and then quit. Having decided this she realized that from that point on she would need to take whatever job paid best— and actively seek those jobs out regardless of the hop-scotch pattern of her career path. When she had saved enough she would leave. For her this was a critical decision point. She freed herself of a great deal of anxiety. She gave up competing for career positions and she came to her decision through a series of logical steps of relevance to her rather than to anyone else.

Another woman who saw very clearly that she did want a career developed a specific plan which included taking a lower-paying job in an area critically important to the career path to the job she eventually wanted to hold. She measured immediate income against potential future income and saw that the payback was considerable. In a sense she invested in job experience rather than in an M.B.A. and in some companies and industries it may well be the best investment.

The absence of clear career goals can lead a woman to allow salary level to be the most critical determinant of immediate career success or failure. While it is always important, this woman would never have made the choice she did if she had made current salary her only criterion.

Career planning is all very well, one might say at this point, and there are some fairly specific questions to be asked in the process. But how do you even go about deciding on a goal years out from now? How can you establish that this is what you will want? Unless you do that, what use are the steps in between?

If this is the case, and it often is, there are a number of important and much more general considerations to bear in mind. The first has to do with overinvestment in a particular technical skill. Where once this served to give legitimacy, confirming a woman's right to hold the job at all, in the future unfortunately it will continue to do just that. Her legitimacy will rest on doing *that* job, not on the more general basis of visible and transferable management skills. Moreover, there is a clear limit to promotions within one function. People tend to move out of them as they move ahead.

Given this, the first step toward goal definition has to be exposure to other functions. What are they? How do they relate to what you currently do? What are the links between production and sales, for example, or between sales and marketing? Between finance and planning? What are the actual job definitions the company has established? Which staff areas would provide the most useful exposure to jobs in the line? Which line areas provide the basic experience this company demands?

The eventual goal, in other words, is established only in outline: advancement, greater responsibility, a series of increasingly complex jobs. The immediate goal is the broadening of one's experience, skill, and visibility to people in a number of different functions. Even more than this it is the expanding of one's work relationships in both number and variety, becoming more comfortable with job changes, and more confident and more skilled at learning jobs one doesn't already know.

As far as the formal techniques of goal-setting and planning are concerned, a number of means exist for developing one's own skills: formal educational programs, in-house training programs; working with a supportive boss or peer in designing a project which requires goal-setting and resource-, time- and action-planning; asking to be a participant in the next planning cycle in one's area, if necessary on one's own time. There are, in addition, a number of useful books on the subject and corporate training departments can often advise and help in identifying them.

Problem identification, problem analysis and techniques of problem-solving are as important to management competence as goal-setting and planning. Most people are willing to solve problems as they occur in their jobs. If they weren't they wouldn't be employed. The special quality which distinguishes a competent manager from the rest is less a willingness to solve problems as they occur and much more the ability to anticipate where they may occur in the future, what they will probably be like and what some of the alternatives are, either for avoiding them or working through them. On the job, a woman who wants to learn could identify a potential problem and try to assess the probability that it will occur. She could analyze its impact if it did occur, who and what would be affected, what would be changed. She could then search for ways of circumventing the problem or resolving it if it did occur. She would need to discuss what she had done with someone more knowledgeable than she, deliberately using the entire exercise as a means of learning. And because problem-solving is an area of skill which must often be applied in a group setting, an understanding of group dynamics and a familiarity with techniques or group problem-solving and group leadership are extremely important. A great deal of research has been done in this area and while you can certainly learn from experience how to deal with group relationships, it is a slow and often difficult process. Learning group processes through a combination of one's own particular experience and the insights one gains from others' research findings helps ground intuition to fact, and a limited ability to anticipate to a broader capacity to predict.

Goal-setting, planning, problem-solving. Skills that can be deliberately acquired and formally learned. Yet their usefulness and effectiveness is often critically dependent on one's working relationships with others—bosses, peers and subordinates.

Who *are* you in this informal system of relationships —a system which must inevitably surround the formal positions on an organization chart? How are you seen? By whom? How helpful, useful, important can these people be to you in achieving the short- and long-term career goals you have set?

Men dominate the informal systems of organizations for the straightforward reason that there are so many more of them. As outsiders to these systems, and thus people with an important interest in not having them operate to their disadvantage, women nonetheless often fail to take them into account in developing a career plan. And women who recognize the system's importance are often uncertain as to how to deal with it. Parts I and II of this book have hopefully added to individual insight and understanding but this must now be translated into action by every woman who wants a management career. This means that women must begin to develop relationships with people in the organization over and beyond those they see in the day-to-day course of their work. They must begin to identify key individuals whom they should get to know in the near future. These are people who will be important in making promotion into and success in the next job possible. Simultaneously women need to establish an informal system of their own, with links to other women in the organization. As outsiders to the men's informal system, women need sources of support, advice and information beyond that system, and one of the most viable means of achieving this is a support group made up of other women.

In order to make this system work, women will have to be willing to set limits on competing among themselves for unrealistic reasons. For example, instead of falling into the trap of competing to be "chosen," with all of its no longer questioned social and psychological overtones, women might recognize that job opportunities for competent women exist, and that the support, help and advice of other women can be extremely important in getting to them. An informal system like this can help women identify job opportunities in other areas of the company. It can help identify male bosses who are particularly supportive of women, who are good coaches and who might be willing to give advice and help to women other than their own subordinates. A functioning women's informal system can be a critical source of information and guidance as well as support.

This issue raises questions that have to do with the ability to trust, to share, to depend on. As outsiders to the system, women have often tried to ensure their own survival by creating a job situation in which they could be wholly and solely dependent on themselves. The outcomes of this strategy conflict directly with the requirements of a management position. At this level the job *is* coordination and leadership of other people and this requires the ability to trust in, depend on and delegate to others, in particular one's peers and subordinates. The leadership of other people demands an ability to depend on and trust in them. It means being able to behave in a way that allows them to believe that you do. It means being able to motivate them by creating a climate that is open enough for them to work and grow within it.

When you have never done it before, the task of trusting in and depending on others seems formidable, for a manager who trusts and depends on others at work must, in a seeming paradox, assign goals, work plans and tasks in a way that is so clear that subordinates cannot mistake the task, its requirements or the level of competence that achievement of the goal requires. Beyond this, a successful manager needs to be available to subordinates in a way that allows them to feel free to come for help, advice and support in the process of meeting the goal assigned.

A willingness to risk dependence on others and thus to delegate responsibility is strengthened immeasurably by the recognition that these issues have nothing to do with a sense of personal trust or personal dependence, that rather they have to do with a willingness to believe a subordinate can accomplish an assigned task effectively because the task is clearly understood.

To get this process under way the structure of reporting relationships must be clear and *consistent* and must be tied to the goals assigned and the responsibilities delegated. You cannot keep changing assignments and reporting relationships or establishing them formally and allowing them to shift informally and still expect consistency. Inconsistency breeds ambiguity, ambiguity breeds anxiety and anxiety breeds mistakes. In their own turn mistakes leave the manager feeling that the original mistake lay in not doing it all herself. This issue is particularly important for women with extensive supervisory experience who are particularly vulnerable to accusations that they can't delegate, that they won't trust others to do as good a job as they would do themselves.

A manager's sense of security must necessarily rest not on being able to do every aspect of the task herself but on the establishment of a clear and effective structure of goals, tasks, responsibilities and relationships and an equally clear definition of performance standards. From this the ability to control the process of goal achievement develops. Performance can be evaluated by reference to every necessary element in the structure: rate and effectiveness of progress toward the goal set, the quality of task achievement, the degree of thoroughness and often the level of initiation in carrying out assigned responsibilities, the clarity and, most important, the quality of the relationships necessary to achieve what has to be achieved.

The quality of relationships is an issue that is too often glossed over because it is difficult to deal with. Yet it is essential to group performance. For the individual woman working in groups predominantly made up of men it is an issue of critical importance.

Finding a style that will work effectively, that doesn't come across as too "masculine" (hard, tough, aggressive, unfeminine) or too feminine (not tough enough, overemotional, too hesitant, not enough of an initiator) is Catch-1001 for women in male work groups. How do you set standards for the quality of relationships you expect subordinates to meet if you are uncertain about the style you should yourself adopt? If nonetheless you try to, how many conflicting signals will you send? How much uncertainty will you convey—and cause?

In Part II we looked at twenty-five women who made it to the highest management levels of their companies. We looked at the style they adopted in their twenties, and how it changed in their thirties and forties. In their twenties their style emphasized competence and task achievement as the major reasons for a work relationship. In other words they de-emphasized the personal aspects of their relationships at work by indicating a high priority for objective task achievement and the reasons why they sought to do this are still real.

Often an extremely competent woman must develop a working relationship with a man, and he can be boss, peer or subordinate, who challenges her right to be there. He may systematically attempt to force the relationship into traditional masculine/feminine roles. He's a leader, she's a helper. She's a woman, not a manager. When this happens the best strategy she can use is to keep bringing the issue back to the job to be done. Persistently. Consistently. Presenting herself as someone whose central priority is the highest level of task achievement, she gives him two choices: either to accept her premise as the basis for the relationship or to withdraw. If he withdraws he makes it clear that for him task achievement is far from a major priority. This may ultimately prove a source of considerable embarrassment to him and if he still persists he may even damage his own career. Through it all, if you are the woman involved, you need to keep the closest guard you can on how you feel. Don't get angry. If you do, don't show it. Anticipate that incidents will occur and think through beforehand how you will deal with them. When they do happen, you gain a few seconds of valuable time by being able to say to yourself, "Here it is again, I expected it. And it's happened and no doubt it will happen again. So why don't I get on with the job?"

If these incidents typically occur in a group in which you are the only woman (and they often do) it is even more important not to respond. If you do, hoping for support from the other men in the group, typically you won't get it. At best you will get silence from the others, and that won't help how you feel. At worst one or two will actively support your attacker, particularly if you respond in a way that seeks to put him down.

So don't respond. By not responding, by ignoring the incident, you relieve the others of a burden they don't want and typically won't accept—which is to support your own necessarily defensive challenge to their concept of themselves as men. They will leave you to fight this battle alone because, in front of you, a woman, they're not going to do each other in. If you want support from men on this issue you will find you get it not by asking for it, but by proving you can weather the strain.

This example leads directly into the issue of male groups, their tacit rules, their implicit function and their structure.

One implicit function groups perform for their members is to confirm a sense of shared identity—and to affirm a sense of individual identity by enhancing one's sense of self-esteem. *You* are a member, *you* are a part of this group, *you* belong, *you* share the group's identity—and it is a two-way street: in sharing the group's identity you seek affirmation of your identity in ways which contribute to your sense of self-esteem. The status of the group, its reputation for achievement, its exclusivity are all important in determining the extent to which you want to share the group's identity and simultaneously be able to affirm your own.

Now think carefully: status, regard, recognition, influence; the group can help make them all more real and individual self-esteem benefits. Is it real that society has sent us a message through most of our lives about the unequal status of men and women? Is it real that woven through this message there is the complex issue of sexual as well as social status?

A woman joining a male group for the first time: Is there an implicit challenge to the status of masculinity itself—sexual, social, intellectual? How will a group of men respond?

Depending on a man's own feelings of status security—sexual, social and intellectual, with all of their complex interrelationships—his response may range from welcoming a newcomer with potential brains and ability, to curiosity as to whether she will make the grade, to a need to test whether or not she can, to—in the worst cases of primary sexual insecurity—a determined attempt to put her back where she belongs, to drive her out, to maintain the status of the group as male, as masculine, and thus avert the threat to a precarious sense of masculine sexual identity which the presence of a competent woman evokes.

Unfortunately most men don't cluster around the first part of the continuum. Fortunately neither do they cluster around the last. Instead they scatter across the middle and this means that certain identifiable norms will prevail in the group's behavior.

A woman's presence will change the group's identity. The group is no longer all-male. The traditions we have grown up with mean that a woman's presence will be seen and felt (not necessarily thought through) as lowering the social and sexual status of the group, thus reducing the identity-affirmation aspects of group membership. Yet this woman may well advance the group's intellectual status. She will in effect be a test of the group's orientation to task achievement. To what extent will they give priority to the task to be done? To what extent will they instead concern themselves with a sensed diminution of the other aspects of their former status? The chances are they won't know —and remember these are not issues which present themselves in a conscious, clearly thought-through form. They are for the most part emotional, self-esteem issues rather than rational ones. So they will test her, and they will test her on all three dimensions— intellectual, social and the explicitly sexual.

The social tests have to do with traditional roles and stereotypes: getting the coffee, keeping the minutes, becoming the "secretary"—sending out follow-up memoranda, arranging for space, getting Xeroxing done, seeing whether she will react more emotionally, even break down in tears. They will play *all* of these games and the underlying meaning is "can we get her to do it?"

Don't play the game. The social role tests most often represent things someone will have to do. Decide which you will do, say so, and say you assume someone else will take on follow-ups and the reproduction of documents, someone else will arrange for space. Don't refuse to get coffee or take minutes. Simply say that they'd better be done on a rotating basis, you'll do them this week, someone else will have to do them next. Don't let these things *become* tests. They have to be done, help allocate them around. Don't lose your temper, stay matter-of-fact and above all don't get so upset over any of them that you break down in tears. The gamesters will have won and you will have lost.

The explicitly sexual tests are more difficult to deal with, particularly if they are attempted by men whose positions are superior and whose influence is important. The first and best strategy is not to engage the issue at all. You don't see it, hear it, understand it. You are so preoccupied with the job to be done that you tend to respond to a come-on with "how much is your area going to be over budget this month?" Think through ahead of time a series of task-related responses you can make in these situations. With practice you may even be able to smile as you make them. Remember that most men's defenses tend to work on a basis of denial: you win some, you lose some, you don't ever really lose everything. So don't believe you're dealing an ego-shattering blow if you turn off the sexual come-on as soon as it is made. Its maker will swiftly recover. The real problem comes when you encourage it. You feel flattered, you like flirting or you get a real kick out of double meanings, blue jokes, stringing him along. Then you try to stop it because it's gone too far and you inevitably do it clumsily. By then his ego involvement may be real, his reaction unpleasant and potentially damaging. Don't let is start.

In cases where the pressure persists and the man holds a more powerful position recognize that you're into something much uglier than a game. If you agree, the line runs, you've got a career, if you don't, you don't. Really? Test it. And test it on the logical basis that if you don't want to become involved you haven't all that much to lose anyway. Keep a log in detail—what is said, when, where, under what circumstances. And let other people know. Not just friends of yours but at least one senior man you can trust. Ask for an appointment with your EEO officer and without naming names at this stage (you refer to a man whose position is senior to yours) cite dates, times, places, circumstances and what was said—what the promise was and what were the threats. Make a formal record of your statement to be placed in your personnel file and write that record yourself. Make another formal request for a job transfer and follow up on it. In the meantime stick it out and maintain all the distance you can. You may never want to sue but if you ever should there are now (1976) successful precedents for it. You will need clear and convincing evidence so keep your own copies of everything you place in your file and keep a list of the names and positions of people who know about the situation, again with dates, times and a record of what was said. Above all stop being afraid, stop thinking there is nothing you can do, that you can't handle situations like this, that the only alternatives are either to give in or to leave. Most companies are run by decent people, and those that aren't, aren't worth working for. If you want neither to give in nor to leave then see that you take the steps needed to ensure you have to do neither.

The intellectual tests are still more complicated because woven through them are both social and sexual issues. For the sake of your own ability to be clear about what you're doing, ignore these other issues. This means ignoring the element of sexual competition or of sexual challenge that often underlies the seemingly straightforward issue of knowledge, skill or experience. Focus on the task to be done. Ignore those parts of a statement calculated to prove that its maker, a man, is cleverer, more profound, has much wider experience, wields much greater influence than you do, and don't get trapped into trying to match them or to show them up as untrue. Concentrate instead on what little—or much—there may be in what he says that helps advance the work to be done and respond to that.

Hopefully a message has come through in this discussion and it is a message that emphasizes competence and task achievement as the basis for establishing relationships with men at work—peers, bosses and subordinates. It is the same message that we saw and heard in the career histories of the twenty-five women who made it. It is a very important message, for the process of socialization and its underlying meaning—for girls, boys, men, women—hasn't changed all that much despite the apparent casualness of attitudes toward sexual relationships. A decision to have a sexual relationship with someone at work is clearly a very personal one and we are not attempting here to discuss the situation of someone who wants one. What we *are* saying is that if you don't want such a relationship, and if you're tested as you will almost inevitably be, there are ways of dealing with the tests which have lower costs attached than others. Even if you do want such a relationship, pass the tests first, establish who you are in terms of your own ability, become a person with skills and a demonstrable level of competence before you decide to become involved. If you don't, you may never get beyond the level "woman." You may spend triple time proving at a different level of innuendo that "in spite of the fact you're a woman" (given that people learn only too quickly of in-company relationships) you really have got brains, ability and competence.

So far we have discussed some very specific things that a woman can do, first to help determine whether she is serious about a management career, second to plan and work through what such a career will involve and third to deal with the difficulties that will arise because of her sexual identity. We now want to look at possibly the most sterotypical issue of all—the management of emotions, of feelings. That there are stereotypes to the point of caricature makes this issue no less important, for there is an element of truth in the stereotype.

Women grow up in an environment which allows them and often encourages them to express emotion freely and openly. It is entirely acceptable for girls to cry. Men grow up learning that it is unmanly to cry, that only sissies show emotions that are not aggressive and hence "masculine." Most men learn early in life to build defenses against expressing those feelings or emotions they have learned to see as "feminine" and volumes still remain to be written about the relationship between this specific cultural inhibition and the staggering increase in the incidence of violence across the social structure.

We don't want to get into this issue here. What we do want to do—placing no value judgments whatsoever—is to consider the impact on individual women of the stereotype many men hold about women at work: that under pressure, when criticized, when attacked women will get so upset, be so unable to manage their feelings, that they will break down and cry.

There is truth in this stereotype. Women tend to express feelings far more directly and in doing so they often make men extremely uncomfortable. For many men, crying in front of other people and particularly in front of other men is the mark of someone who is uncontrolled, whom you can't trust to make the right decisions. In 1972 Senator Muskie cried in the New Hampshire primary and lost his party's support. Good for him, we might say as women, it was not whether he won or lost, but the honor and decency with which he played the game. The question is, what are your goals? In retrospect, if he *had* managed to win his party's nomination, if he *had* gone on to win the election . . . And we can leave it right there. The issue is, if you want a career, how do you help yourself achieve it in organizations made up predominantly of men? How must you be seen and heard? Given the culture and its masculine codes, what must you downplay if you don't want to be seen as foreign to the system?

There are techniques for managing one's emotions and women should learn them. You may never need them, never use them, but they are useful to know. First, sit down and think back over the last few years. What kinds of work situations have caused you to feel or to become emotionally upset? Write them down. Describe what happened; where you were, what the setting was, who was involved, what was said and what, as precisely as you can describe it, made you feel so angry or so vulnerable that you broke down in tears. After you've written this down look for patterns in what you've written. Is there a pattern in terms of time? Is there a pattern in terms of the people involved? Did it tend to happen when you were criticized? When you were challenged? When you felt left out? The more you can understand about why it happened in the past, the more you can anticipate when it may happen in the future—and this is the first step toward managing it.

The technique of identifying patterns in the situations which have caused you trouble in the past, sitting down with pad and pencil and listing all the specifics you can recall, is an extremely useful one. From a clearer picture of the past you can much more clearly predict the future. You can anticipate your own reactions and those of others and think through ahead of time how you will deal with them.

If you can begin to predict, for example, when, in what kinds of situations, under what kinds of pressures you are likely to cry, you can begin to deal with it by recognizing the signals and acting before it happens. You can remember that you have an important phone call coming in to your office and your secretary isn't there. You can simply excuse yourself for a moment and, in privacy, you can either pull yourself together, drink a glass of cold water (which helps) or go ahead and be upset. One further thought and it's a very simple one: if you want to cry you have a right to cry. This helps release a great deal of the tension over "you shouldn't, you mustn't," which most often serves only to ensure that you will. You have a right. What you want to do is be more selective over where you're going to exercise it.

This issue takes us into serious statements. They are all one-liners and women often use them to describe the way they feel. How many apply to you? When you really think about it—against a background of all that we have said so far—what are the career implications of those that do? How difficult would it

208 THE MANAGERIAL WOMAN

really prove to change the directions that these statements imply?

Women describe themselves as waiting to be chosen —discovered, invited, persuaded, asked to accept a promotion. What would it take to stop waiting and start acting? To start letting people know what you want and what you're prepared to do to get it? To let them see you going after it and working for it?

Women describe themselves as hesitant, as waiting to be told what to do. What would it take to stop being reactive and to start initiating? To start asking questions about promotions and job opportunities? To start asking to learn new skills, to be given extra assignments, to take on new projects?

Women describe themselves as often feeling conflicted and confused about their own goals. The process of overcoming conflict involves bringing it out into the open, analyzing and evaluating it, coming to grips with it. Hopefully you can resolve it. Perhaps you may be able to eliminate only one of the conflicting elements. You may even have to decide that indeed it's real and its here to stay. If this is the case you must be willing to conclude that you can and will live with it and that now you're going to get on with the rest of your life. Conflict not understood and not acted upon is an ongoing emotional drain. You feel it, and its physical consequences, without understanding why and often you think that the way to deal with it is to deal with the physical symptoms.

Women say that they become extremely anxious when they have to deal with unknowns. Anxiety does arise when you don't know what you think you should know. Waiting to be told is no solution. If you're anxious, try to clarify the situation. If there are things you don't know, things you need to know, seek out the answers and stop waiting for someone to tell you.

The process of trying to find answers is in itself better than dealing with the anxiety of waiting and hoping someone will do it for you. There is often a fine line here between recognizing that this is what may be happening and converting your anxiety into resentment because "they" haven't done it for you—haven't advised you, kept you informed, let you know. Are there real reasons why they should?

Women say that they find criticism difficult to deal with. Start asking yourself why you are so personally vulnerable. What do you think you have failed to do? Why are you so deeply affected by it? Do you hear it as a criticism of who you are rather than understanding what is said as a possibly valid and objective comment on a particular piece of work? Have you failed to balance criticism by crediting yourself with the things you *have* done well? Men's defenses work far better for them on this issue. Their sense of vulnerability has less to do with a feeling of personal failure and much more to do with the power and influence of the critic. This leaves them that much freer to take corrective action. Beyond this their judgments and criticisms tend to be less personal so they hear the judgments of others in less personal ways. One woman told us she finally realized that men regard a man who has come up with a stupid idea as simply having made a stupid suggestion. She said she suddenly realized she had always thought (and sometimes said), "What an idiot he is!" If you are doing this, stop it. The less personal and the more objective you are in your own criticism of others the less personally and the more objectively you will tend to interpret their criticism of you.

Women describe themselves as reluctant to take risk. If you're afraid of risk ask yourself why. Do you see risk only in the negative? Do you think of risk as an uncontrollable gamble rather than as an accessible and manageable act? Do you think of risk as allowing the situation to determine whether you lose the dime or get it back with a prize? Have you ever thought of risk-taking as something over which you might have a certain degree of *control?*

Think about a career-related risk you might take. Make two lists on paper. The first should list the positives that might result, the second the things that could go wrong. Are there entries on both sides? Do they tend to balance? Does one list or the other seem stronger? Put some odds on your entries. How possible, probable, likely, certain do they seem? Why? What might you do to increase the degree of certainty or decrease it where you don't want it? How, in other words, can you begin realistically to deal with your own assumptions about risk?

Women often say that the only way they can deal with their feelings of guilt over having a career is to try to be a perfect woman/wife/mother simultaneously. How hard have you tried to keep your career life and your personal life totally separate? You've tried fairly hard and it seems logical to do so, doesn't it? There really are basic conflicts between a woman's ability to build a successful career and to be a successful wife, girl friend and/or mother. Listen to the inconsistencies. There *are* conflicts. The problem is that many women believe that the logical way to deal with them is to show everyone including themselves that they are perfect in both roles. Then neither they nor anyone else can criticize them in either. Think of the costs of this strategy. And make still another list. In separate columns list everything you do at work and at home. List the hours, the tasks, the responsibilities, the concerns you are trying to manage and then see whether it is humanly possible to continue to maintain the separation you have striven for. Instead of saying that you are a person who has a career, is a mother, a wife or a friend, you may find you're saying that you're several totally separate people, one person in your career and quite different people elsewhere, each defined as a separate role with quite separate sets of emotional, task and time commitments. If this is the case, how do you deal with emotional conflicts, time conflicts, task conflicts between roles when you have taken such pains to establish them as entirely independent of each other?

You may have to give up your strategy of separation, for it is both time-consuming and conflict-laden. As a man does, you may have to negotiate between roles, trading off time and energy in one today for time and energy in another next week. You will need to do this consciously and deliberately.

To begin, you will have to discuss the responsibilities you have at work with your husband, or whoever else is involved in your personal life. You're going to have to discuss what you do, what the costs are, what the rewards are, what your plans are, what your dreams are. You're going to have to make an explicit effort to have other people in your life understand the commitments you have to make, their importance and the time they require over and beyond the responsibilities you carry at home. If you haven't begun this process it is critically important that you do. If both of you are pursuing demanding careers, a realistic discussion of the demands on each of you can lead only to the conclusion that household responsibilities have to be shared and, if it doesn't, you're going to need to reassess your own priorities entirely.

Reaching a workable conclusion on how best to share these responsibilities may take longer than you bargain for, but particularly if you have children, you should start the discussion immediately. On a day when a child is ill, it may be extremely important that you be at your desk or at a meeting. Your husband could stay at home. But if you've never communicated to him how responsible your job is, it's illogical to expect him suddenly to understand why on this particular morning anything is different from the way it's always been.

Studies of women who enroll in continuing college education programs show that many of the women who fail in these programs are women who have never discussed their goals with their husbands. The husbands never really understood why their wives had gone back to school and the wives on their own had attempted to maintain the same level of housework they had been accustomed to. In contrast, women who succeeded in these programs, some of whom were high-risk students, reported that they had discussed their goals at great length with their husbands and that their husbands had played an important supportive role, taking over a number of household responsibilities to balance the demands going back to school placed on their wives.

The message is—discuss your career with the people who're important to you in your personal life. Recognize that the strategy of separation is a lose-lose strategy. You will have to be clear on how you order your priorities and on what trade-offs are possible. Perhaps some things at home will have to be let go. Perhaps household help can relieve some of the burden. Perhaps your children, as well as your husband, can take more responsibility. Discuss it and work it through. However difficult, it will prove even more so if you don't.

The single woman confronts a quite different level of these problems. While many women and men subscribe to a fantasy that single women avoid all of the shared responsibility difficulties, every woman who is single will know that this is only partially true. The married woman has at least fulfilled all of the traditional expectations. The single woman has yet to do so and she is far more vulnerable to the conflicts this can present. If you are single you are open to the accusation, by yourself and others, that you have failed as a traditional woman. You must deal with the possibility that your career may prove a stumbling block to potential partners. Conflict over who he wants you to be and who you are and want to be is often real. The costs of the femininity/achievement conflict are high—almost every woman needs to assess whether the way she is trying to deal with it might not be made simpler if she were to take a different look at what she is doing—and at her goals, both stated and unstated.

It is after all going to be a long time before the men's world of business becomes anything like a people's place of work. Millions of women will spend an entire career life living and working in a culture whose traditions, rules and implicit codes are derived from the male experience. The extent to which as women we can understand this culture, and manage our existence within it, will determine how far we can go and what costs we will pay. We have always had to work harder and we will continue to have to do so. But let us learn if nothing else that hard work in the absence of goals and workable plans to achieve them remains just that—hard work.

There is a limit to the amount of energy each of us has to spend, and as outsiders to the culture and mores of organizations we have often spent it unwisely. Our unawareness of how organizations work and the limiting set of assumptions we have traditionally brought with us have left us sometimes paralyzed, sometimes frustrated and often angry at what confronted us. We have tended to center our hopes on the way things should be rather than on the way they are and we have as a result been ready to believe that if we met the formal tests of performance we would be justly rewarded. Many of us have been deeply disappointed with the results of this strategy and we have often placed the blame for what we perceive as failure on ourselves or on the men with whom we work. The outcome has been damage to our own sense of self-worth and increased feelings of anger and hostility toward others. Some of us have simply given up trying. Yet the facts are that we can learn. The issues have to do with *learning* and it is never too late to begin.

If we were going to a foreign country for an extended stay we would all agree that it would be more rewarding if we could speak the language of the people who live there. We would try to learn what kinds of behavior were considered polite and what would be considered offensive. We would want to behave in ways which would win us friends. We would want to fit in and to be understood. We would want to know what the country's currency was worth in relation to our own and we would study maps, read guidebooks or perhaps a history or two so that we understood what was there, what we could do, where we could go.

We would figure out the best ways of getting from place to place and we would plan trips, selecting places to visit and mapping out routes. At first we might hire guides to help and then as our confidence grew, we would strike out on our own.

We would try to identify organizations and individuals who might be helpful to us and we wouldn't hesitate to use them if they were needed. During the early part of our stay people who understood our own language would be extremely important. We would seek them out to help us translate what we heard.

We would anticipate that we would often feel frustrated. It wouldn't surprise us if sometimes we even felt frightened and lonely. After all, we would be alone in a foreign country.

If a friend traveled with us, there would be support in there being two of us. If we had a friend living there it would help even more. We would expect to have difficulties, we would probably do our best to anticipate them and so be ready to deal with them when they arose.

And all of this we would accept because we were undertaking an understandably difficult and challenging venture. We wouldn't blame ourselves or the people we met for the problems we encountered. We might think that in our own country we did certain things better but there would certainly be aspects of the country, its culture and its people that we would admire. We would know that we came from one tradition and they from another. We would know that no matter what our histories and guidebooks told us there would be subtleties we could only learn when we got there. We would train ourselves to be alert to the nuances of what we saw and heard, and we would be careful to behave in ways which would allow us to learn more.

Yet when we really wanted and needed something we would struggle to be understood. We would tell people what we wanted repeatedly until we got it. We would struggle with the language until we sensed we had been understood. We wouldn't assume for a minute that by being a nice foreigner trying hard to fit in we would necessarily get what we needed.

In undertaking the journey we would know from the beginning that we would have to learn a great deal.

We would expect to work hard before we left and even harder after we got there. We would recognize that all we learned before we went would only help us get under way once we arrived. We would know we would have to learn even more once we got there. We would know that without plans for what we wanted to do during our stay, a great deal of our time, energy and resources would be wasted. We would know that we wouldn't be able to do everything we would like to do and we would set priorities to ensure that we did what we wanted most. We could realize that we might have to adjust our plans because of situations and circumstances we hadn't anticipated and we would be prepared to change when we had to.

No matter how inadequate we might feel when we arrived, we wouldn't feel guilty about it, nor would we feel that there was nothing we ourselves could do for we would have gone armed with all kinds of resources as well as the belief that we would improve our knowledge of the language, our understanding of the people, and that we would grow steadily in our ability not simply to live in an entirely foreign culture but to enjoy it.

You may want to reread this story. It is the best analogy we can think of for what as women we need to take with us into management careers—for the way in which we need to see ourselves, the organizational culture, its people, the tasks to be done, how to prepare for them, how to carry them out, how to grow in skill and competence, and how, over and above all of these things, to enjoy it.

12

Corporations and the Men Who Manage Them

There are many things which women can do to help increase their own and each other's career success. But what can men do to help women? There are good reasons for men agreeing that more women should be included at all levels of management but there are equally powerful reasons why they may not want to help them get there. How effectively corporations and their senior managers respond to the problems of implementing equal opportunity will determine how many women will move up in managerial careers and how quickly and at what cost or benefit to men, women and corporations.

In order to discuss corporate action, we must first clearly define equal opportunity and affirmative action. It is not necessary to discuss equal opportunity legislation and legal definitions here. Thousands of pages have already been written on the subject. The operative definition lies in the answer to this question: What are the real goals of equal opportunity and how can they best be achieved? Most corporate leaders

218 THE MANAGERIAL WOMAN

believe that *legal* equal opportunity exists now in most corporations. They are right. Most corporate leaders honestly believe that the most qualified person should be the one chosen for every job opening. They would behave punitively toward individuals or groups within their company who openly or actively negated such a policy. All equal opportunity means is that anyone who is qualified can apply for a job opening and must be considered for it.

The critical issue facing women and minorities (any outsider to corporations) is no longer the *lack* of legal equal opportunity; it is one of gaining equal ability to take advantage of it. They and corporate senior managements must now deal with the reasons why, for many women, legal equal opportunity does not ensure *real* equal opportunity. Having the right to a job is not the same as having the ability to get it.

Unless we begin training larger numbers of women to be able to compete successfully with men, equality is unobtainable. Corporate leaders *must* understand that corporate settings automatically favor men and that if women are to compete equally they must be given the opportunity to learn what their male colleagues have often learned automatically. Affirmative action then means taking those actions or creating those programs which can enable women to make up for the set of differences described earlier in this book —differences in perception, knowledge and skill which so directly affect their career success. It means providing financial and educational assistance that will enable women to participate in formal education, on-the-job training, special corporate training, individual boss coaching, and internship and attachment programs. Here women must be able to learn both the objective knowledge and the behavioral skills which they need to be on an equal footing with their male peers.

Women who are competent, motivated and achievement-oriented can convince men in middle management of their right to be supported. The ability of women to demonstrate their competence and potential, however, depends on there being sufficient numbers of them specifically trained to compete in an environment which presently favors men.

Top managements of corporations must also ensure that line managers understand the differences which women are bringing to the setting, and how they as managers can help women to develop. As the people who are immediately responsible for selecting, training and promoting women and minorities they have the most direct control over women's access to career opportunity. They are primarily white men in middle management positions. Despite the existence of legal equal opportunity and its formalized support by senior managers these men are the ones who directly control access to it. Corporate senior managers can motivate these men to open that access, or frighten them into closing it off. Men in middle management must also be told that it is their top management's decision that time and management resources be committed to making women equally competitive. Senior managers must ask that performance evaluation systems be designed to identify and reward a manager's success at training and promoting women. It is all these training needs which most directly define the meaning of affirmative action.

In reality, the question of whether or not women will eventually be included in the hierarchies of American corporations is already moot. The most serious issue before corporations is whether that inclusion will take place because it is imposed upon the corporation by an outside agency or whether it will be voluntarily achieved. An imposed program guarantees that the corporation will be assigned prescribed goals and time-tables for promoting women. These will be accompanied by fixed standards, quotas and procedures for their achievement. A voluntary corporate program which is effective and sincere may convince outside agencies that imposition is unnecessary. This process of convincing is one which must not only convince the external agency but also the women who presently work for that organization. Often the outside agency is brought into the company not by its own initiative but in response to a petition or request of women employees of that company.

Companies which are already operating under a legal settlement (or consent decree) face an entirely different reality than the company that remains as yet untouched by externally imposed solutions. In one major utility, top management no longer asks how many women should be promoted and by when. It struggles with how it can meet the goals and timetables which it has been ordered to meet. In this company, managers at all levels are confronted with the problem of identifying immediately which women employees have the highest management potential and how in the short space of time provided they can become able to perform the jobs to which they must be assigned.

Four years ago we conducted interviews with men and women in such a company. The company had just agreed to a consent decree and the men and women were asked to discuss their concerns about the implications of it. We recall vividly one woman who said:

"I've been with this company for eighteen years. I've worked hard and I deserve to be further along than I am. But now I'm afraid that what's going to happen to me is that instead of progressing logically in my own area of expertise I'm going to be forced into a promotion in a job area I don't know anything about. I'll just be a number, and I'll be robbed of the feeling that I earned a promotion. I may be promoted over a guy who's been working for years in his area to get the job that I've just moved into. If all this happens I'm going to get hurt. I may have to leave the company. It seems ironic that something which is supposed to specifically help me has such a potential for hurting me."

In contrast, one man spoke poignantly about his own concerns. He said:

"I've thought about this over and over. I'll tell you where I come out. I believe that there are lots of good women in this company. They should be higher than they are. I've decided that I can live with losing out to a gal who is really good— at least as competent for a job as I think I am. But, honestly, I don't think I'm going to be able to cope with a less competent and experienced woman having it ahead of me. And to tell you the truth, that's what I think is going to happen. And if it does, I'll fight it."

Imposed solutions put severe pressure on both men and women in a company and this pressure may well be destructive to them and to the productivity of the company itself.

Another reality faced by companies with imposed solutions is that in times of poor business conditions and changing technology, promotional opportunities may narrow but they must continue to meet goals and timetables. Consequently almost all promotions at all levels must go to women and minorities. Some women will be put into dead-end career paths which offer no long-term future. Thus in meeting its immediate goals the company faces the ironic situation of creating serious longer-term difficulties for itself and the women so affected.

The climate which results from imposing solutions for affirmative action is not a very positive one for men either. The backlash or *negative feedback* potential from men in a company is very high. Since that backlash can seldom be applied directly to the obstruction of the promotion of women it can only result in a more subtle obstruction of motivation and productivity in the company as a whole. Men don't need to obstruct women's promotional opportunities in order to preclude a large number of them from progressing. They need only fail to recognize the existence of their potential and hence fail to train, develop and support their professional growth. Once operative, this kind of backlash is difficult to identify and even more difficult to counteract.

Recognition of the numerous negative implications of imposed solutions provides thoughtful corporate leaders with strong impetus to undertake immediate and extensive voluntary activities, activities which will ensure not only equal opportunity, but equal access and, most importantly, true affirmative action for the women in the company. It seems clear that the short-term higher cost of developing successful voluntary affirmative action programs must always be less than the combined immediate *and* longer-term economic, managerial and personal upheaval of imposed ones.

Historically the ways in which corporations dealt with the issues most critical to the implementation of affirmative action too often only exacerbated preexisting negative situations. Senior managers of most American corporations saw the issues relating to equal opportunity and affirmative action as ones which could be voluntarily resolved by the personnel department. Unfortunately, the average personnel department's inability to achieve equal opportunity only ensured an imposed solution.

In fact, the implementation of equal opportunity is a line management issue. To implement it means first creating and instituting a corporate policy which all managers will be held responsible for implementing. The policy must be converted into goals for how and by when women will be able to begin to prepare themselves for moving up. These goals must then be communicated down the line and tied to a reward and punishment system for success or failure. All of these actions must initiate from top management. Senior managers will also have to recognize that middle managers are overworked.

In recent years, in addition to their already full-time jobs, middle managers have been required to become responsible for the management development of minorities and women, the management of ecology and the management of corporate social responsibility. Each of these has been defined as an area of responsibility to be *added on to* rather than somehow integrated with the ongoing middle management job. Middle managers are undertrained for these new responsibilities. There is little hope that they can or *will* be able to train any numbers of women for management careers until their ranks are expanded, their resources increased and their training improved.

In addition, many senior managements have failed to insist that the role of staff departments must be to assist line managers in performing their jobs, rather than to substitute themselves for part of the line managers' responsibilites. The selection, development and promotion of employees is a primary responsibility and accountability of each manager. Yet many corporate managements have abdicated large parts of that responsibility to staff departments. One of the very real results of that error is the inability of the mangers in those corporations to respond directly and effectively to the task of developing women and minority subordinates. Equal opportunity for these people can never become a reality until senior managements return this responsibility to line managers and hold them accountable for doing it well.

The only area of equal opportunity implementation which can be usefully segmented to a staff department is that of planning and implementing immediate affirmative action training programs. Meeting imposed goals and timetables frequently forces a company to go outside its own pool of women employees in order to obtain enough qualified women. With voluntary training programs and learning experiences many more of the women presently working for a company will become able to compete for advancement in it. This avoids both the backlash and demotivation of longer-term women employees. The fact that the majority of these women are known, committed, and have in-depth business experience *must* make them the more desirable and profitable employees to upgrade and advance first. The results of these programs will be the creation of a pool of candidates for promotion who should and must be able to meet the requirements of each line manager and who compete freely with each other to be chosen. It is at this point that staff departments must withdraw from the equal opportunity process. Theirs becomes a responsibility to help the line manager do what he or she is now accountable and responsible for doing. Requests for further help must now initiate from the line.

An imposed approach to achieving equal opportunity will, by its very nature, come into conflict with many of the ways of doing business which are natural to a particular company. It will supersede all company policy and lines of authority. It will certainly come into conflict with that company's normal method of developing and promoting people within it. While some forms of this conflict can lead to useful improvements the same positive results can occur from voluntary responses and without the cost which imposed change always extracts. The greatest danger of an imposed solution is that it leads to the creation of even more special agencies to respond specifically to the imposed solution. These agencies then generate special processes to implement the solution, working against any eventual integration of the individuals involved into the ongoing organizational system by becoming themselves blockades to the mainstream of corporate activity.

Voluntary responses to affirmative action and equal opportunity allow a company to generate those responses from the strengths of its particular organization. A company can make use of its ongoing procedures, departments, and line management system. It can improve the general quality of its managerial performance as it works toward responding more effectively to its equal opportunity goals. In making its management more responsible for and more responsive to the development of women and minorities it can gain the added benefit of improving the entire process of subordinate training and promotion within the corporation. It can be very creative and industry-specific in developing its affirmative action programs. It is free to choose those methods and activities which it feels are best suited to its particular organizational structure and style. Both the women and the company benefit from this process.

The integration of new groups of people into the permanent ongoing structure of an already formed business organization requires permanent change in the organization itself. Success at it therefore will also require changes in basic management practice. Only those corporations that are willing to undergo such basic and permanent change can hope to achieve real equal opportunity.

We have emphasized the importance of the role that a middle management man can play in making the implementation of equal opportunity successful. What is it that we must understand about him and his role? How can corporations motivate him to support the development of women subordinates and how can women also encourage him? Most of us, men and women, fail to understand the depth of the issues which both the present quality of corporate life and the inclusion of women into its managerial ranks raise for men who manage. All people are products of their upbringing and at east partial reflections of their cultural heritage. Each generation has the propensity to act out some of the collective rights and wrongs of earlier generations. Few people ever become fully aware of the foundations of their prejudices and stereotypes and most people don't even realize how many they have. Fortunately many of the negative actions of men toward women are more the result of unquestioned assumptions than of almost unchangeable prejudice. Many of the things men do which have negative results for women are motivated not by hostility toward women but by our historic cultural demand on men and the male group that they ensure their own traditional role survival. Consider the background of many of the men who are today's corporate managers.

During the 1950s and early 1960s millions of white men took jobs in American corporations. Those men went to work, accepting the then given set of rules, expectations and promises for their future. Soon after they went to work the Black movement began and as the result of social pressure and federal legislation corporations across the country were motivated to achieve an accelerated inclusion of Black men at every level of employment. As a result, the original promises, hopes, expectations and rules that existed when those white men went to work were changed. Their opportunities were narrowed, their expectations had to be lowered, their aspirations modified, as the degree of competition which they would face increased. Although it was painful, many men found ways to agree that it was right and just and somehow they accepted those changes. They recommitted their energies to their jobs and went on with their careers. And during this period, top managements in this country never once acknowledged for those men that it was true that their opportunities might now be more limited. They never accepted that those men had a sense of pain and anger about it and that they had a right to their feelings. In fact, legal threats resulted in senior management responses that insisted instead that all was well, that nothing had changed and that equal opportunity had always existed. Then top managements issued written policy statements much like what follows:

> We are and always have been an equal opportunity employer and it is right and just that we continue to make every effort to include minority workers in this company. It is true and desirable that this may increase the competition at all lev-

els. Every good employee should welcome this change for it will ensure that the most talented and able people at every job level will have to be the ones who are chosen for promotions.

The irony in this statement is obvious. The white males' legitimate fear that competition had increased was not only confirmed but it was exacerbated. It was as a result of these early and naïve corporate actions that male backlash became a reality.

No sooner had this generation of white men made an adjustment to all of the changes which the Black movement brought to their own career lives than the women's movement began. More legislation was passed by the federal government. Executive orders were issued from the office of the President of the United States which legislated specific equal employment opportunity for all women. Once again American industry tried to open its doors for the drive toward accelerated employment. And that same generation of white men, many of whom had now achieved positions in management, saw that their opportunities, hopes and dreams would again have to be narrowed, modified and even lowered. This time, as middle managers, they would also be the *specific* people who would eventually be held responsible for locating, training and promoting the very group that was the new cause of this threatened loss.

Many men in that generation now feel confused and even hostile, bitter and angry. Within the context of their particular experiences they have an absolute right to those feelings. Yet few top managements in this country have taken any action which would signify to those men that they understand and acknowledge those feelings. Few top managements in this country have seen the need or accepted the responsibility for saying to those men: "Gentlemen, your feelings are very painful. But it takes a great deal of energy to be angry, bitter and hostile. In investing that energy this way you have nothing to look forward to but further unhappiness. One way or another, women and minorities are being and will continue to be included. Gentlemen, we issue you a challenge. A challenge that accepts that, in spite of those feelings, the reality is upon us. We must include minorities and women. Our choices are few. But one which we all share is whether it is imposed upon us by agencies and groups outside of this company or because all of us collectively, men, women, majority or minority, agree to a cooperative effort. And we make such a commitment because we share the belief that what is right and just must be made real. It is our challenge and our opportunity to be the ones to do so.

"If you have the energy to invest, wouldn't you rather invest it in such a way that you can live out the rest of your career with a feeling of having contributed to a building process? Wouldn't you forgo anger and bitterness if you could achieve a feeling of having contributed toward a permanent improvement in the quality of life at work? The reward will probably not come to our generation but certainly to the generation of our children. Gentlemen, wouldn't you rather spend your energy that way? Whether 'they' will be included is not a question. The only question which faces all of us now is how that inclusion will take place—by force or choice?" That few top managements have been willing to acknowledge in some form the need to deal with the feelings of the white men who work for them, that few have perceived that corporate success or failure in implementing the inclusion of outsiders is critically dependent on this acknowledgment is testimony in itself to the state of the quality of life assumed to be adequate in the majority of American corporations.

Whenever we talk about an issue that concerns expanding the numbers of people who will compete in a setting so critical to every individual who has to work there, we are talking about a very human subject. A subject which touches very deeply the personal beliefs, assumptions, values and emotions of every individual involved. Yet American corporate life has grown so structured and task-oriented that emotion is seldom considered a legitimate influence on its activity or of the people who work for it. It is as if upon entering the door of his/her place of work every individual must leave behind those critical aspects of himself/herself which deal directly with his/her basic humanness. We see the stifling results of this condition when we are confronted with a corporate issue touching on those feelings which in the context of the organization are illegitimate. The corporation then becomes immobilized. There is no corporate or management modus operandi for dealing with people at an emotional level.

We believe that it is critical that all people, men and women, minority and majority, who participate in or are considering participating in management careers take this issue very seriously. The quality of life in most American corporations has disintegrated into a way of life which is almost wholly instrumental.

The American society has set as one critical definition of masculinity the achievement of high position in corporate leadership. We have seen the development of a parallel set of assumptions which lead men and women alike to believe that management is man's rightful world. People in this society have tended to believe that to achieve the highest positions in corporate life is to have truly succeeded as a man.

Similarly, our society has taught its boys and men that to be seen as a successful man, one must never acknowledge or exhibit emotion in professional life, one must encourage other men to deny and cover up these feelings too. From earliest childhood children learn that little boys must not be emotional because if they are they cannot become successful men. Seldom are they taught the difference between being sincerely sensitive to another person's feelings and the undisciplined expression of emotion.

It is healthy and natural for all persons, men and women, to live directly in both the instrumental *and* the affective worlds. The best example we can give to explain what we are saying here is to quote the man who said, "My boss is the best boss I've ever had. When you go in there and she criticizes your work she makes sure that you leave feeling that you are a good and valuable *person* who wrote a bad report." It is healthy, creative and productive for men and women to express feelings as well as ideas and to use instinct as well as logic. When we consider the desirability of acknowledging the feelings of bitterness, anger and hostility in a generation of men that has been asked to absorb hundreds of years of social injustice we must be encouraged to believe that if the feelings of those men could begin to be acknowledged perhaps then it will not take so much convincing and challenging to convince them of the need to work as hard as they can to ensure the inclusion of the people who will insist that the world of work be more humane. Perhaps if these men can come to experience working with the people who have been forced to live as outsiders to American corporate life they will be encouraged by the discovery that many of these people have been able to maintain a greater sense of humanity. Perhaps these men will realize and even support the idea that if "outsiders" can be included in any numbers at all levels of business management there will then be a greater hope for improving the quality of work life.

In practical terms, this could mean that an employee's family responsibilities could be brought more into balance with work demands. It could mean that paternity leave could become a basic part of a young father's life. Transfers and relocations could become voluntary and the refusal to accept one could not close out a person's future. It could lead to career paths which do not need to be vertical to be seen as successful. It could free up a person who loves his/her job to stay in it without a stigma being placed on him or her. It could result in work climates that encourage individuals to experiment and learn and grow beyond their defined job responsibilities. It might even unlock the upper limits of productivity and lead to a new surge of creativity in American industry. At the very minimum it will lead to more people being healthier and happier at work. Men must begin to decide where they really want to stand on this issue. The world will be a better place for more people if men join in supporting these demands for a better quality of life at work.

Many people have also been too free with the accusation that men are a prejudiced group who individually and collectively have stood in the way of women. They have been suspected of joining together to sabotage women who have tried to succeed at the management level. Certainly there are men who are prejudiced against women. There are also men who are personally threatened by competent women and who will act to defend themselves. But are these actions the actions of male chauvinism or those typical of any threatened person? There are individuals and groups everywhere who hold prejudices against other individuals and groups. There are even women who are prejudiced against other women. We have been encouraged to find as we've worked with men in management across this country that few are truly prejudiced against women. Many react negatively toward women in the professions as a result of the assumptions they hold about who men and women are supposed to be. And many women share and reinforce those same assumptions. They have never been stimulated to question them as they have lived out their adulthood. It is particularly encouraging to find assumption rather than prejudice because if we can present people with new, logical and objective data that question the ways they have perceived and acted to date, they are often willing to change their assumptions. In contrast, prejudice is seldom if ever affected by fact.

Our observation of the men in corporate managements is that most are good and decent people, who not only manage American industry day by day but also care a great deal about the women to whom they are married and the daughters whom they are raising. There are many men who are sincerely trying to understand what it is like to be a woman in this society. Yet many men find themselves, at mid-life, having spent all their working years pursuing career achievement in order to achieve what they and their society have defined as part of successful masculinity. Now these men have begun to see highly competent women performing the same work. This evidence raises a series of issues for these men which are exceptionally difficult for any adult person to cope with. We know that having ability to achieve in management careers is not the result of being born a man, but how does a man whose career success has confirmed for him his masculine identity now give up this confirmation? Can he even be expected to try?

Many men in industry will behave defensively toward even the idea that there are many women in our society who are as capable as most men of performing competent executive work. Many women do the same. Sadly, most people in our society have failed to try to understand this. Contemporary men are no more responsible for what our society has spent centuries defining as successful masculinity than are women, and women are no more responsible for what we say is successful womanhood than are men. Ours is now a shared responsibility for beginning to understand what our cultural inheritance has been. Both men and women have tended to define themselves in part by their differences. What a man is is what a woman is not. That, in itself, has tended to mute, cripple and narrow all our abilities to live up to our potential as human beings. That we have incorporated occupational roles as a major part of that defining process is sadly destructive.

The reality of today and tomorrow is that most people who work will work because they have to. In the future more and more people will have to work in order to survive. As that pressure increases on all people, our need to free occupational roles from gender roles will grow desperate. Perhaps the key to how all of this can change and change with the support and acceptance of at least the majority of men and women in our society is to focus our thinking on what we want the world of work to be like for our children. One American ethic which seems to continue with force is the commitment of the parents of every generation at least to try to improve the world for their children. Certainly the quality of life at work is an improvement they are due.

In our professional work, we have often spent many hours convincing a man in management that it was important for him to try to understand the differences which women were bringing to the organization setting. He would respond to our argument by repeating again and again that he agreed that men and women are different but that he thanked God that they are. He would agree that women are less successful in management careers but say thank God that is so. Finally, we would ask him whether he had any children. If he said, "Yes, I have a son and a daughter and they are very different," we would say to him, "Tell us the answer to just one question. If you had known on the day that your daughter was born that starting at the age of twenty she would have to work continuously to survive would you have done anything differently with her than you have done up until now?" Most of these men would be stunned by this question. We recall vividly one corporate senior vice-president who lowered his head for a moment and then looked up at us, staring but not speaking. We had to ask him what he was thinking. He said, "I don't *think,* I *feel* sick to my stomach. If she has to work, then I've done it all wrong." Even a man like this is not usually prejudiced, just terribly certain that his own assumptions about men and women are correct.

After studying present statistics, we believe that over the next twenty-five years, a majority of the women in our society will have to work for economic survival at some period in their life. Most of them will have to work continuously for their survival. If we consider the following statistics we can see the basis for this conclusion. Today, in 1976, about half of the women of working age in this country work. Of the women who work almost a quarter are heads of households, responsible for supporting themselves and at least one dependent. Of the women who work over a third have children under the age of eighteen and almost a quarter under the age of four. Among married couples, where both the husband and wife work, a large majority probably could not meet their fixed monthly debt obligations without some dollar contribution from the wife's salary. Current divorce statistics if projected show us that over a third of the women who marry in the late teens and early twenties will be divorced and self-supporting by the time they are in their early thirties. The birth rate is 1.7 children per couple and still falling. And with the introduction of sophisticated methods of birth control children can be planned and scheduled to fit in with and to complement career and personal life plans. When the Equal Rights Amendment is ratified it will eliminate discriminatory alimony policies which have been enforced in many states in this country. Support will be awarded only where clear circumstances warrant it and it is equally possible that women will be asked to support men. Child support will be seen as a mutual responsibility. Women who are able to work will contribute to the support of themselves and their children. It seems to us that these trends point in only one direction. More and more women will be working because they have to. Hence, men will have to accept women in careers and will be competing with women who, like themselves, work because they have to.

Men have told us time and again that their career motivation derives in large part from knowing from early childhood that they would have to work all their lives. They say that knowing that they would also be responsible for several other human beings merely increased and solidified this pressure. The support of a family motivated them to get as much as they could from the career they knew they would have to have.

If this is true, then women who will have to work to support themselves and others will also become more motivated to achieve higher positions, higher pay and greater responsibility. And so, after it is all said and done, the issue of the inclusion of women into the managerial ranks of modern organizations is probably not just an issue of social justice, or legal justice, but in the end it becomes even more basically an issue of economic justice, an economic justice which derives from the need to survive.

In reality, American industry must begin to realize that it is confronted less by the immediate threat of legal action or even social judgment and far more by the longer-term implications of the economic needs of women and the probably concurrent inability of industry to provide enough opportunities to employ all the people who will need to work. Corporations should be realizing today they are confronted with a serious future labor problem. Undoubtedly, the eventual response to a society in which more people may need jobs than there are jobs will have to be one in which economic survival is based upon the division of a collective input. This is not meant in any way to suggest a radical political or social change but rather to suggest that the context of the American family may change to the extent that whichever partner is either best able to work or most wants to work will work and that at different times different members of the family will become the primary wage earner and that need not always be a man. In many family units economic survival will demand the input of all of its members even if the end result is that each will earn somewhat less. In other words, more jobs paying less money may have to be created if we are faced with a slowly expanding gross national product. And a temporary reduction in the standard of living in this country may be a necessity. An acceleration in the rate and size of growth in the gross national product may in part depend on corporate success at including larger numbers of people. Access to previously excluded groups may provide the single most critical source of new creativity for American industry. Undoubtedly, therefore, the final response will be to divide work and its rewards more evenly among a larger number of people. The concept of the four-day work week may well become normal practice. The idea of even a three-day work week may be soon to follow so that in any given work week there will be more jobs for more people—each of a shorter duration and carrying a lower economic reward.*

But if our society and, in particular, the managements of corporations become so deeply embroiled in trying to create instant responses to what they perceive as "the immediate threats of women," they will miss the critical issues of the future. If they miss the issues they will fail to identify the accompanying problems. Consequently they will find themselves totally unprepared to respond to those problems with viable solutions. In our work with the top managements of a few extremely enlightened American corporations, we spend as much of our time in trying to anticipate and project what the long-term and most serious problems will be as we do in implementing immediate programs. This allows us to measure and evaluate our choice of immediate solutions in terms of the degree to which they will help us to move toward solution of the longer-term and more critical issues.

Today's issue of equal employment opportunity may well be tomorrow's issue of equal right to survival —survival as individuals, families and corporations. If this is what we all face in our future then the need for

* A longer-term drop in population may eventually ease this situation. However, no immediate relief will be felt.

the cooperation and coalition of employers and employees, men and women, majority and minority is clear. Ours is a joint problem which only we, together, can hope to resolve. We can no longer afford the ease of self-definition that we get from measuring and maintaining the differences between us. We must struggle to find the strength of our common humanity and, working from that shared strength, move forward to attack those issues which threaten all of our rights to a just, decent and rewarding work life.

Notes

WHAT THIS BOOK IS ABOUT

1. U. S. Department of Labor, Employment Standards Administration, Women's Bureau: *Women Managers*, February 1972, and *Women Workers Today*, July 1975.

CHAPTER 4

1. Gregory Rochlin, *Man's Aggression*. Boston: Gambit, 1973, p. 20.
2. *Ms. Magazine*, Vol. II, No. 3, September 1973.
3. Eleanor Maccoby and Carol Nagy Jacklin, *The Psychology of Sex Differences*. Reprinted by permission of Stanford University Press, 1974.
4. Ibid., p. 151.
5. Ibid., p. 160.
6. Ibid., p. 161.
7. Ibid., p. 157.
8. Ibid., p. 157.
9. Ibid., pp. 157–58.
10. Ibid., p. 158.
11. Ibid., p. 154.
12. Ibid., p. 172.
13. Ibid., p. 211.
14. Ibid., pp. 351–52.

15. Ibid., p. 368.

CHAPTER 5

1. Margaret Hennig, *Career Development for Women Executives*. Doctoral thesis. Harvard University, Graduate School of Business Administration, 1970.
2. See "Personality Correlates of Vocational Planning" by Rosalind Chait Barnett, in *Genetic Psychology Monographs*, 1971, 83, pages 309–56. Reprinted by permission of The Journal Press.
3. D. V. Tiedeman and R. P. O'Hara, *Career Development, Choice and Adjustment*. New York: College Entrance Examination Board, 1963, p. 84.
4. E. C. Lewis, *Developing Women's Potential*. Iowa State University Press, 1968, pp. 11–12.

CHAPTER 6

1. Margaret Hennig and Barbara Hackman Franklin, *Men and Women at Harvard Business School* (unpublished M.B.A. research paper).
2. Elizabeth Douvan and Joseph Adelson, *The Adolescent Experience*. New York: Wiley, 1966, p. 81.

CHAPTER 7

1. Elizabeth Douvan and Joseph Adelson, op. cit., pp. 247–50.

CHAPTER 8

1. Margaret Hennig and Barbara Hackman Franklin, op. cit.
2. Donald E. Super, "A Theory of Vocational Development," in Peters and Hansen, *Vocational Evidence Development*. New York: Macmillan, 1966.
3. D. V. Tiedeman and R. P. O'Hara, op. cit.
4. Rosalind Chait Barnett, op. cit.
5. M. S. Horner, "Femininity and Successful Achievement: Basic Inconsistency," in J. M. Bardwick, E. Douvan, M. S. Horner and D. Gutman, *Feminine Personality and Conflict*. Belmont, California: Brooks Cole Publishing Company, 1970, pp. 45–76.
6. Theodore Rosenbloom, *A Study of Middle Management*. Unpublished paper. Iowa State University, 1965.

Index